ENDORSEMENTS

"It's never too late for the perfect marriage.

I know what you're thinking. A perfect marriage? Not possible. Not with my spouse.

And there you have it. And that's why I can tell you that Don McCulloch's book, *The Perfect Circle,* should be on your reading list.

While we may not believe that a perfect marriage is possible, we all know what it might look like. Don challenges his readers to take another look at their own relationships. He provides help, encouragement, and hope. If you've been married for a month, or for decades, your marriage will profit from Don's words of wisdom and insight.

Based on Dr. McCulloch's years of practical, Biblical counseling experience, he has brought together a down-to-earth, godly, and usable approach to improving your marriage. His information and step-by-step counsel will give you practical ways you can use immediately to reanimate your relationship with your husband or wife. From the first chapter, you will be given tools that are functional from day one.

The book is written to husbands. On purpose. But if you're a wife, you will also benefit from Don's expertise and teaching.

Believe that God wants your marriage to be the best it can be. And then pick up *The Perfect Circle* and practice what's inside. You'll be as close to a perfect marriage as you can get."

-Ron Benson, Pastor, Grace Community Church,
Bay City, Michigan

"A very helpful guide for a Christ-centered marriage with many practical suggestions to deepen it relationally, emotionally, and spiritually. In an age in which male passivity in marriage is a common problem, this insightful book from a seasoned counselor offers a way forward."

-Paul Copan, Professor and Pledger Family Chair of Philosophy and
Ethics, School of Ministry, Palm Beach Atlantic University,
West Palm Beach, Florida

"The *Perfect Circle* captures the current tension men face between societal pulls to self-satisfaction and a biblical sense of authentic intimacy and covenant in marriage. Dr. McCulloch reminds us that being in relationship with our wives is about the process much more than the outcome. He provides men a map of how to build an "island" to face the challenges in loving our wives with the intense intimacy that Christ

loves the church. Dr. McCulloch, in this book, has started a conversation that I hope men will participate in."

-David J. Van Dyke, PhD, LMFT, Associate Professor & Director of MFT program, Wheaton College, Wheaton, Illinois

"Don has done a good job addressing some of the issues that married couples face today. I believe it's pertinent to focus on the role of the husband/father in a separate book. The premise that men are basically angry and women are depressed that their marriage is not living up to their expectations or God's standards will give you the opportunity to evaluate your own relationship in a meaningful way."

-Jonathan Oldham, Executive Director, Harvey Cedars Bible Conference, Harvey Cedars, New Jersey

"Great stuff-- like being invited into Don's counseling office to hear insightful and practical ideas I can start applying today to our marriage."

-Ryan Brasington, Worship Pastor, Rio Vista Community Church, Fort Lauderdale, Florida

"With transformative principals and key questions, Dr. McCulloch has written a book that finally provides practical tools for the husbands of today's culture. After being captured by the excellent introductory chapter, I desired to delve into the six tasks Dr. McCulloch skillfully described. By understanding the creative Christ-like role of husbands, we may wisely become islands of successful and joyful marriages."

-Dr. Brent A. Gray, Director, Spanish River Counseling center, Boca Raton, Florida

"The absence of male leadership in the home has become an epidemic in our day. Not only does Dr. McCulloch put his finger on the right family issue, he also gives us men what we really need: good practical biblical instruction on how to lovingly lead our wives. As a pastor, I am thankful for this book!"

-Tom Hendrikse, Sr. Pastor, Rio Vista Community Church, Fort Lauderdale, Florida

PERFECT CIRCLE

A HUSBAND'S GUIDE to THE SIX TASKS of a
CONTEMPORARY CHRISTIAN MARRIAGE

DON MCCULLOCH, PH.D.

Wasteland Press

www.wastelandpress.net
Shelbyville, KY USA

Perfect Circle:
A Husband's Guide to the Six Tasks of a Contemporary Christian Marriage
by Don McCulloch, Ph.D.

First Printing – March 2013
ISBN: 978-1-60047-843-7

Printed in the U.S.A.

0   1   2   3   4   5   6

For Gwenn

CONTENTS

INTRODUCTION:
Perfect Circle

Her little ring is a little thing, but it's all I could afford. Now she's mine, all mine till the day I die, and I never wanted nothin' more.
—Kenny Chesney from "Never Wanted Nothing More"

Love is a losing game.

—Amy Winehouse

I have attended many weddings in my life, including my own, and every one of those weddings involved the groom giving a ring to the bride. In the majority of those ceremonies, the pastor commented on the meaning of the ritual. The ring, which has no beginning or end, symbolizes eternity. Therefore, the ring makes the statement that marriage is a "forever" event. Marriage is not to be broken. The ring's circular shape also conveys strength while the preciousness of marriage is symbolized by the expensive metals used to fashion the ring. So the ring is the perfect circle and the hope of a perfect union at the beginning of marital life.

In reality, people today are cynical about the survival of any marriage. When we hear of an engagement, we become London bookmakers, predicting how long this one will last. If that is an overstatement, it is probably fair to say that a majority of folks fall somewhere between Ken Chesney's lyrics, "all mine until the day I die" and the late Amy Winehouse singing "Love…is a losing game."

We are mired between eternity and despair. Contemporary marriages face at least three major challenges—the devaluation of marriage in society, misunderstandings about basic emotions and the fall of mankind, and a lack of knowledge about basic building blocks of a biblical marriage.

The Devaluation of Marriage

The institution of marriage has changed dramatically in the last few decades. Prior to the 1970s, divorce was relatively rare. Now the United States has about a 50% divorce rate which is the second highest in the world. This creates an atmosphere that works against the concept of "until death do us part."

One strong contributing factor to marital impermanence is the age at first marriage. In 1970, it was 23 for males and 20 for females. In 2010, it increased to 28 for males and 26 for females. This five to six year increase is significant. Marriage delay usually means an increase in cohabitation and sexual experimentation. Research indicates that a greater number of sexual partners and cohabitation prior to marriage are both correlated with an increased risk for divorce[1].

However, the worldwide phenomenon of marriage delay among young professionals has another downside. It is emblematic of how society views the concept of marriage. In the past, marriage was spoken of as a life goal. Young women stated openly their primary desire was to get married and have children. This sentiment is now rarely voiced. Instead, careers and personal fulfillment are the new primary goals for both men and women.

Since eighty-six percent of women in their 20's rate marriage as a high priority, marriage is still highly desired. However, many aspects of life usually associated with marriage; companionship, sex, and children can be acquired without actually getting married. There is very little social censure anymore when these aspects of life occur outside of a traditional marriage arrangement. Marriage has switched from a revered and desired public institution to one of private choice, and as a choice, can be kept or simply set aside[2]. This is most seen in American celebrity culture where marriage is considered either undesirable or a highly fluid arrangement.

These factors all play into the psyche that the marriage ring is not really meant to last forever. While it is easy to complain about changes in society as a whole, Christians have been equally poor in maintaining marriage as a forever event. Evangelical Christians have long been noted for focusing on "feelings" or the subjective in their approach to faith. This longstanding complaint by hardheaded intellectual secularists carries some weight in how some Christians have approached marriage. Christians have desired marriages that conform to subjective and personal ideals of a perfect marriage. They have their own private notion of the perfect circle. Unfortunately, these ideas were not always based on biblical concepts of marriage but more about personal needs and expectations. Similar to the secularists, when those certain needs or expectations were not met or fulfilled, Christians made the same choice to set marriage aside. Or to divorce and then remarry with the hope against the odds that needs and expectations might be met in a new marriage. This should be obvious based on the discontent sowed by endless hours of life comparison on Facebook and scanning dating sites.

The ideals that constitute the perfect circle may be different for Christians, but sadly they are no different statistically in their divorce rates (it should be noted that divorce among a minority of Christians who follow a conservative pattern – less sexual partners than average, no cohabitation, less delay in marital age, no previous marriages and, this is key, active church involvement, have divorce rates much lower than 50 percent).

Given the commonness of divorce, it is instructive to note the reasons given for the ending of "forever" marriages. The most common reason for ending a marriage is infidelity. This is not surprising. Infidelity is certainly a violation of the covenant of marriage and is the one reason listed by our Lord Jesus Christ as grounds for divorce. What is surprising is that the next most common reason given for divorce is not communication problems, sexual incompatibility, money issues, or abuse (which are all in the top ten), but the rather vague notion of "no longer being in love." [3]

Marriage is one of the greatest ways to express love. The marriage ceremony is a public symbol of that love. Yet, the feeling of love that surrounds an engagement, a marriage ceremony, and a honeymoon is impossible to sustain for years on end. For some couples, the feeling of "no longer being in love" happens early in a marriage. For others, a long slow drift away from those original feelings occurs. When marriage is based on subjective feelings, there is always a creeping sense that certain needs and expectations are not being met, which eventually corrodes feelings of love.

While marriage remains popular, society does not value marital permanence. A large contributing factor to the devaluation of marriage is the shift in the meaning of marriage from a noble life goal to a personal choice that is based on feelings. Fortunately, this is fixable. However, it requires a whole new understanding about the meaning of marriage. This book provides six tasks for contemporary Christian husbands to perform that change the way marriage is valued and understood.

Basic Emotions and the Fall of Mankind

Men get angry and women get depressed. That is the reality a husband must deal with if he wants to transform his marriage. That is not to say that men don't get depressed and women don't get angry, they both experience these emotions as well. Poor marriages, however, seem particularly rife with angry males and depressed females. The reason for this phenomenon may be traced to the first few chapters of the Bible.

Initially, our first parents (Adam and Eve) lived in a state of harmony and sweet communion with each other and with God their Creator. After the fall into sin, a curse was pronounced by God on mankind. The curse pronounced, among other things, disharmony between men and women until this present day. Specifically, Genesis 3:16 contains this phrase, "…and the woman's desire will be for her husband and he shall rule over her."[4] This pivotal passage sums up the root problem in every marriage.

The woman has a "desire" for her husband. She has an emotionally driven and sometimes irrational way she wants her husband to act. She sincerely wants her husband to be the man she thought she married. This desire tempts her to try to control her husband. Her controlling behavior leads to the opposite outcome.

The man resists her control and does not meet her desires. Instead, he is tempted to be angry with her. Eventually, he may use angry words and even physical force to dominate her. This is the husband's problem. Just like his wife, his problem is emotionally driven and sometimes irrational. In his case, the temptation is related to the "shall rule over her" part of the curse. He is angry that she is trying to change him.

Eventually, she gives up and resigns herself to not having her greatest needs, desires, and dreams met. She becomes depressed.

In my office, I observe this pattern over and over again with couples seeking help with marriages.

Our parents and their parents dealt with these same issues. Family histories shape and mold our behaviors and our expectations in marriage, but history is not the root problem. Personality types play a role by highlighting the need for control and the tendency toward either anger or depression, but they are not the root problem either. These and other factors only exacerbate the pattern. Ultimately the true problem is the curse. The curse must be reversed! The curse must *specifically* be reversed in the dynamics of our marriage. Curse reversal leads to marriage transformation.

Interestingly, the solution to the curse is mentioned in God's pronouncement of the curse itself. Genesis 3:15 states, "he will crush your head and you will strike his heal." Most theologians consider this passage to be a hopeful prophecy concerning Jesus and Satan—the fallen angel who instigated the fall of man. Jesus will crush Satan, and Satan will strike Jesus' heal. This prophecy was fulfilled on the cross. Jesus was wounded, but the first crushing blow to reverse the curse began with Christ's transforming resurrection. Jesus is the solution to the curse! Only God can forgive sin, and only Jesus' redemption can transform marriages and the effects of the fall.

Husbands have a unique role to play in this process. They must resist the urge to become angry with their wives, instead modeling the love of Christ to them. Husbands must model all of the pertinent biblical images of Christ to transform their marriages. Through Christ, and through a husband who embodies a Christ-like approach to his marriage, the desire of the wife's heart is fulfilled. The curse is thereby reversed. This fulfillment in marriage, although imperfect, is part of the process of helping a wife stop controlling her husband, and start letting go of desires related to the curse. This creates a new pattern in which marriage is supernaturally transformed.

The Basic Building Blocks of a Christian Marriage

As a psychologist and marriage counselor for over twenty years, I have noticed that wisdom and knowledge do not always go together. Both wisdom and knowledge are needed for a successful marriage, but bright people sometimes make stupid choices. To some degree, it is understandable. There currently exists a second generation of men who grew up without a good biblical model of what it takes to make a marriage successful.

In essence, *Perfect Circle: A Husband's Guide to the Six Tasks of a Contemporary Christian Marriage* is the advice I would want to give my own son or any married man who desires change. It is my hope that the tasks in this book will form the basic building blocks of great Christian marriages. Despite the title, nothing is perfect or easy. I do not see this book as a "how to" manual, but more of "why not try these tasks?" and see if it doesn't lead to lasting positive change.

Each of the following chapters describes one crucial element which allows the curse to be reversed and marriages transformed.

The first task begins with *Invitation.* The husband invites his wife to the marriage of her dreams. Every trip down the aisle to exchange rings begins with an invitation. The invitational approach models what Jesus accomplished in saving His bride, the church. This approach also provides the motivation for marriage transformation. When the husband is the one who takes the first step in changing marriage patterns, a successful outcome is most likely. Usually, the wife has already been unsuccessful in her efforts to bring about change. The husband holds the key to marriage transformation.

The second task is centered on a new approach to *Showing Love*. Marital love must model Christ's love in a manner very different than the type of love found in many failing marriages. Failing marriages are founded on a search for self-fulfillment and reciprocity. Couples evaluate their marriage in terms of what they are getting out of the relationship. If the amount of return from the marriage is greater than the amount of effort required by the marriage, then the marriage is judged to be a good arrangement. The foundation of such marriages is the concept of reciprocity—I should get at least as much or more than what I give. The second task completely reverses this concept by not counting the cost of love. Respect and love are given without regard to what is being given back in return. Most basically, the second task of marriage is for husbands to treat their wives with love, regardless of whether there is a perceived return on investment.

The third task involves *Leadership*. For this task to be accomplished there needs to be understanding in the marriage regarding the male role. Many husbands have no sense of the masculine role in marriage. Often roles are exaggerated characteristics of either domination and control or a frustrated withdrawal from family involvement. The default mode for most husbands is passivity which serves as an imperfect defense against angry emotions. The six tasks in this book provide a model for spiritual leadership that is balanced and Christ-like—a model in which a husband becomes the spiritual prophet, priest, and king of his marriage. This type of leadership is real, but it resists the physical "ruling over" aspect of the curse.

While the first three tasks require a husband to be proactive, the fourth task requires a husband to be reactive. Everything of great value needs to be protected. Every successful marriage requires boundaries and the avoidance of anything that would threaten that relationship. The fourth task is to *Avoid Temptation*. There are certain things that have no place in the perfect circle.

The fifth task is to *Nurture Significance* in your spouse. Both men and women suffer from low self-esteem and negative feelings of significance. Despite all the societal messages that tell us to feel good about ourselves, it is still a prevalent problem in contemporary marriage.

Women especially suffer from negative self-evaluation. The feminist movement provided a way for women to be treated as equals, excel academically, athletically, and in the workplace, but it has not been able to provide feelings of worth and significance. Women often tell themselves they are greatly lacking in a major area of life. If they excel at work, they believe they are lacking at home. If they are doing well at work and in the home, they believe they cannot compete with idealized and completely unrealistic standards of physical attractiveness. The connection between a wife's negative evaluation of herself and depression is obvious. Husbands have a unique role to play in reminding their wives that they are fully loved and accepted by God. This is accomplished by the husband nurturing his wife's sense of significance in Christ.

The final and sixth task requires the husband to *Deal with Anger and Depression*. Husbands often deny having problems in this area, but when problems do exist in this area and are not addressed, the perfect circle looks more like the broken dysfunction of a reality show.

If these six tasks are consistently completed there is the real possibility of reversing the curse and returning to something much closer to perfection.

To help prepare for a presentation about these six tasks at a men's retreat I chose to put the first letters of the tasks into an acrostic: ISLAND. "I" is for Invitation, "S" is for Showing Love, "L" is for Lead Your Wife, "A" is for Avoid Temptation, "N" is for Nurturing Significance, and "D" is for Dealing with Anger and Depression.

Was it a spiritual coincidence that this spells ISLAND? I don't think so. Again, "husbands must model all of the pertinent biblical images of Christ to transform their marriages." In essence, we reverse the curse in our marriages when we model Christ and his gospel of love and grace. Whenever a Christian husband models Christ's gospel of love and grace, that husband is attempting to build an island paradise out of his marriage. Of course, if you have ever watched the TV show *Survivor* then you know this is not easy.

The Bible often uses farming analogies that speak of hard work. Creating an island paradise is also hard work. It requires complete dependence on our heavenly Father to help us. But the picture of living on an island paradise in the midst of a turbulent sea that is modern marriage is certainly motivating.

In writing *The Perfect Circle*, I have solicited feedback from my clients, my counseling students, my university peers, my Sunday school classes, my friends with good marriages, and my church leaders so the book in your hands is both unique and ultimately transformative.

The Perfect Circle is based on real life clinical experience. It allows the reader to be a "fly on the wall" in the counseling experience of my clients who have succeeded in creating transformed marriages. Examples are also given from my own marriage of almost thirty years, no less transformed by these concepts.

The Perfect Circle is based on biblical principles related to marriage, including the pivotal concept of love and respect. Biblical, spiritual, and psychological principles combine to offer every reader a chance to create a marriage that is transforming in a way that reverses the curse on marriage. When a husband proactively seeks to complete the *Six Tasks* he is likely to create the marriage of his wife's dreams—that marriage soon becomes a husband's dream marriage as well. In the process, it transforms the marriage into one God will bless.

Of course, women may also read this book and benefit from knowing the six tasks of transformation. However, transformation most often occurs when husbands take the initiative.

Also included is an Appendix containing a list of resources I have seen positively impact the couples I have had the privilege to counsel. While not always agreeing with all the authors have written I still believe they serve as valuable resources.

THE FIRST TASK:

Invite Your Wife to the Marriage of Her Dreams

A good marriage is where both people feel like they're getting the better end of the deal.

—Anne Lamott, *Joe Jones*

Becky stood at the kitchen sink. Her hands moved back and forth, sloshing the warm soapy water that cleaned her dishes. The vague heat rising from the sink and the din of the kids arguing over the television in the background sent her into a reflective mood. Becky thought about all the years she had quietly pushed Eric to become more involved in their marriage. Eric had been so aggressive when he was pursuing her before their marriage. He had clung to her as tightly as the apron that now hung around her waist.

She placed a finished plate in the dish drainer. It seemed Eric had become more passive and distant as the years of their marriage ticked past. She was not the type to nag. She politely asked for his involvement. There were rare moments when she was more direct and would complain, especially when she needed help with their kids. She felt guilty when she did complain because he was a successful businessman who worked hard to provide a comfortable living for her and the kids. Just running her hands over the polished granite counter that surrounded the white ceramic sink was ample evidence of Eric's provisions. All of her efforts to engage her husband in family life seemed to make him more frustrated and even less involved in the marriage. She didn't want to admit it, but she was falling into a depression because she had not found the marriage of her dreams.

That was before Eric attended a men's group at church. She couldn't believe the changes she had seen in him since that day.

Date Night

Becky laughed as she put another dish in the drainer. She could still see herself standing half in and half out of the garage the day Eric came home from the men's group meeting. She could smell the grease and dirt on her hands. She had been repairing her son's bicycle tire and was dressed in her "gardening" jeans and a stained t-shirt. Her hair lay dull and flat against her scalp.

Eric arrived home and suggested they go on a date in a couple of hours at their favorite restaurant. This was certainly unexpected. She made an Olympic effort to get dressed for a night on the town. Her hands burned from rubbing them so hard in an attempt to remove all the grease.

The ride to the restaurant involved the usual silence. Eric's face was so stern when they finally sat at the table that Becky began to dread what he was going to say. She suspected he was going to say he wanted a divorce or maybe his company was asking him to move again. Instead, he asked her what the marriage of her dreams would look like. At first, she did not know what to say. She had been telling him her desires for years and now he was asking her what they were. She took a breath and decided to go for it.

"I would like you to call me every single day and just ask how I am doing…and then listen, just listen, without telling me what to do," Becky said. "I would like you to come home with a smile on your face. I would like you to ask me, 'How can I help you?' and then happily do whatever I suggest, as if it were important to you, as if Harold your boss were asking you. I would like you to put the kids to bed on time without me even suggesting it. I would like you to take me out dancing at least once a month. I would like you to leave me little suggestive note cards, like you used to. I would like you to take me out to buy clothes and suggest options and give me your opinion. I would like you to initiate sex without fear of rejection. I would like you to make a second effort the next day if I do reject you. I would like you to read the Bible out loud every night at dinner."

The sudden quietness of the house startled Becky from her daydream. The television had been turned off. Eric had taken the kids to bed. As she stood up and walked out of the kitchen, Eric came down the stairs with a big smile on his face, "The kids want *you* to read to them." She playfully grabbed his arm, like some tag-team event, as she brushed her body past him on her way upstairs. As she climbed the stairs, Eric looked up at her asked, "Is there anything I can do for you while you take care of the kids?"

Becky's response was delayed by the half laugh, half smirk that involuntarily took over her face. Her marriage had been so transformed she was giddy over putting the kids to bed. Eric indeed had fulfilled every item on Becky's list. He invited his wife to the marriage of her dreams.

He took the lead in his marriage after a man at the group challenged him to do so. Eric didn't know what that looked like, so he asked the man. "You need to ask her what she desires in your marriage, and then follow through," the man said. His advice worked.

Eric and Becky were clients of mine who transformed their marriage. As their marriage counselor I can take little credit for their success. In fact, I learned something from them. Eric and Becky's transformation cause me to reflect on the importance of invitations in my own life.

As an adolescent, I loved tennis. Being self-taught, I honed my skills by practicing against the wall of the community center. Adults would sometimes play on the adjoining dilapidated black asphalt court in the evenings. Most afternoons, I was a solitary figure; the whack-whack drone of my ball hitting the wood frame wall and then bouncing off the cement only to be endlessly returned. Imagine my excitement when I learned our town had its own summer league team for junior high boys. The invitation to leave the obscurity of the community center and join a real tennis team was a relatively small but life changing event.

Playing on the tennis team led to an invitation a few years later to work at a summer Bible conference where they needed tennis coaches. Working at the Bible conference led to my love of the Bible and counseling. Invitations beget invitations. In this case, invitations shaped my future.

Invitations come in a variety of forms. In high school, they arrived by phone. I admit to waiting by the phone many Friday nights for friends or girls to call. Today invitations might come via email or Facebook. Young people make sure their instant messengers are in receiving mode. And let's not even get into text messaging.

Of course, I remember the invitations that I didn't get in high school and college: the parties I missed and the girls I didn't date. Invitations inevitably have to do with belonging and not belonging. The person who is wanted, important, and considered with esteem is the one who gets the invitations. That's exactly why invitations are so important within a marriage. They convey and bestow those same sentiments on our wives. Invitations imply that she is loved, wanted, important, and worthy.

One of the most important Bible verses on marriage is found in Ephesians 5:25, which says, "Husbands, love your wives, just as Christ loved the church and gave Himself for her..." In this context, the passage refers to Christ's sacrificial love which husbands are to emulate. That sacrificial love is also demonstrated by the invitational *way* Christ loved the church, His beloved. We often see God actively seeking and inviting His beloved into relationship with Him.

In modern evangelical church experience, we often think of God inviting nonbelievers into relationship with Him through an altar call at the end of a service. For many people, this event was the beginning of a relationship with Christ; however, the moment of salvation is not the end of God's pursuit of His beloved. We can look at Jesus' statement to Zacchaeus, "Today salvation has come to this house, because he also is a son of Abraham; for the Son of Man has come to seek and save that which is lost" (Luke 19:9-10). Jesus is seeking the lost, but the lost in this case are the children of Abraham with whom His father already had a relationship.

If we look at how Christ related to the people, we see examples of his invitational approach. In the parables, He tells of people being invited to great feasts; elsewhere, we see Him not forbidding the children to come to Him. We see direct invitations to those who might follow Him.

The most poignant picture of this concept is found in Revelation 3:20, "Behold I stand at the door and knock..." This passage is often used as a call to initial salvation; however, Christ is knocking on the heart's door of His *own* church. These are people who know Him well, yet Christ knocks at the door to invite his followers to deeper intimacy. The implication is that we, His beloved, don't seek that intimacy—instead, Christ invites us to intimacy.

The invitations are sent, but they are often not heeded. They are rejected out of hand, and then made light of or ignored (Matthew 22:5). They are rejected with excuse (Luke 14:18-20), or even violently rejected (Matthew 22:6). The meaning of these parables, that God invites and His people reject, is clear.

This theme is important to our marriages. Christ invites and pursues the beloved despite regular rejection. This is not a new theme. God is compared to a jilted lover in the Old Testament. God is often portrayed through a love relationship with His people, Israel, who in response continually pursue adultery (as objectified through their idolatry). This is a theme of the book of Hosea. God is pictured as trying to "allure" His people (Hosea 2:14). He says, "That you will call Me, 'My Husband', and no longer call Me 'My Master'" (Hosea 2:16) and "I will betroth you to Me forever." Despite these words of tenderness and longing on the part of God, His beloved is unfaithful. Other examples of this sentiment are found throughout the Old Testament (Genesis 34:3, Judges 19:3, and Ruth 2:13).

God's approach to His beloved is continual invitation in this lifetime. Despite rejection, God continues to pursue His beloved because He is a covenant-keeping God. A Christian husband should demonstrate, in like manner, the same kind of zealous pursuit of his beloved in the covenant of marriage. This is the beginning of a transformed marriage.

So, how does a husband love his wife as Christ loved the church? He copies God by being sacrificial and invitational. God pursued a relationship with His beloved. He already had a relationship through the covenant, but He pursued a greater level of intimacy, despite resistance and rejection. Our wives dream of a marriages with such greater intimacy.

Joe Namath, the Hall of Fame quarterback for the New York Jets, is noted for the quote, "The best defense is a good offense." Apply this concept to your marriage. If your wife complains about your marriage and criticizes you, then don't play defense. Go on the offense and begin to invite her to the marriage of her dreams.

Why should you pursue her dreams? Successful leaders know that transformation requires motivation. At first, she will be motivated if you invite her to the marriage of her dreams. Once that is established—and change may come easier than you think— you can both begin the process of making sure the vision for your marriage is mutual. If her dream is one that God intended and would bless, you may enjoy her dream so much that you will wonder why you didn't go in that direction years earlier. Do not stubbornly resist your wife's dream for marriage out of pride. Change always works best in an organization when it flows from the top, or where the power originates. That means change is often up to the husband. When men respond to the call to invite their wives to a better marriage, the desired result is almost always produced. On the other hand, wives can rarely force their husbands to do what I am suggesting.

Let me give some practical suggestions on how to put this principle into place:

1. **Invite your wife**. The pattern for inviting your wife probably started when you began dating. Invitations were not supposed to end there. The invitational approach should be an attitude, or a lifestyle of daily interaction with your wife. The Bible prophet Hosea talks about God's allurement of His beloved (see Hosea 2:14). How can husbands invite, pursue, and even allure their wives in practical ways? Begin with your attitude. Banish selfishness and think of her interests first. This one will be tough. It may mean weekends without golf, football, or NASCAR. Find out what your wife would like to do this weekend, and invite her to do that activity with you. This will be a switch. Imagine her reaction when you say, "Honey, would you like to go to the craft show this Saturday?" Later on, ask her to play golf with you. If you show a genuine interest in the things that matter to her, she might consider joining you for recreational activities, or she might feel fulfilled and be happy to have you play golf with your friends. Watch your tone in conversations; be polite.

Be the kind of person to whom you would want to talk. Your wife may not be talking to you simply because your tone is not inviting. Jesus drew others into conversation.

2. **Know your wife's interests and act on them**. If your wife's dream is to go on a trip to a foreign country, surprise her with the tickets, or just invite her to go and do the planning together. Invite her out to dinner at that restaurant she has always wanted to try. Invite her to a weekend at a Bed and Breakfast that she would find romantic, even though the idea might be appalling to you. And then, enjoy yourself. Laugh and have a good time. If you do not really know your wife's dreams, or if she cannot put them into words, invite her to a brainstorming session where she lists on paper what a dream marriage would look like. Having her write out her picture of a dream marriage can be an affirming and encouraging experience. Developing mutual dreams, which I call "envisioning," can energize the most stagnant of relationships.

3. **Take the first step**. Initiation can be tough. Initiation is something that many men fear with exceptional loathing. For many a successful man, the thought of rejection is psychologically unbearable. I can't easily explain why this is, but I have observed the threat of initiation. First impressions are often indelible. When I was a wet-behind-the-ears freshman at college, I met my friend who I will call Barry. Barry, a high school decathlon champion, looked more like a man (he was a sophomore) compared to my high school kid appearance. He also dated a beautiful young woman. I met them both in the library. My first impression was that Barry had everything: looks, brains, build, and the girl. I felt lucky to be his friend. However, impressions can be deceiving. As I got to know him better, I realized that my idol had the same insecurities and weaknesses all men have. He was a great athlete, but only an average student (I never did see him much in the library after our first meeting). He broke up with his girlfriend, and he spent the next two years of his college life paralyzed by

the idea of having to ask out someone else for a date. Despite his obvious ability to cast a positive image, he possessed no self-confidence in the initiation department. I watched him become physically ill if he had to call a girl on the phone. Half the female population at my small college would have loved to date him, but he couldn't make the first move. The incongruity of this situation is striking, but it is an ironic reality. Many "mover-shaker" CEO husbands are frightened of initiation. Perhaps they fear the possibility of rejection, or perhaps they fear conflict might occur. Even if you are like my friend, begin the process of inviting your wife to the marriage of her dreams. At this point, a husband should see the genius of inviting his wife to the marriage of her dreams. Inviting her to dress like a Victoria's Secret model and to serve beer while you watch television nonstop will not go over well. Putting your wife's interests before your own is actually a biblical principle that God will honor (Philippians 2).

As husbands, we need to live by faith and trust God for transformation. This means that if initiation is uncharted territory, like Abraham leaving Ur for the desert, husbands need to take that first step in faith. Your wife may or may not initially respond positively, but the principle for transformation—inviting your wife to the marriage of her dreams, remains in force.

When I received the invitation to play on the tennis team and to work at the Bible conference I felt like I was on cloud nine. In marriage, husbands have an opportunity to create those same feelings. Eric did this for Becky. It does not have to be complicated. It could be little things: Would you like to go to church on Sunday? Shall we go clothes, grocery, or hardware shopping together? Would you like to eat at that new restaurant you mentioned last week? How about we go out for coffee and just talk about whatever you want to talk about?

Key Questions

1. In what activity or place does your wife want to participate or visit? What would make her really happy?
2. If you don't know what would please her, are you willing to ask her tonight?
3. What has been holding you back from asking her about her dream marriage? A lack of faith, selfishness, or simply fear of the unknown? Pray about this process.
4. Is initiating activities with your wife more or less difficult than initiating activities with business affairs? Why?
5. Would inviting your wife to what she wants put your relationship in a better place?

THE SECOND TASK:
Show Love

And now these three remain: faith, hope and love. But the greatest of these is love.

—1 Corinthians 13:13

I am a big fan of the *Lord of the Rings* movie trilogy. One of my favorite scenes is when the good King Theoden of Rohan is awakened from his thralldom by Gandalf. He had been put under a sleeping spell by the evil Saruman and his lack of responsiveness has led to dire consequences for his kingdom and family. This is an instructive analogy of husbands who have taken a passive approach to marriage.

Husbands are to be the spiritual kings of their families. Their mission statement is "love your wife." This clarion call is expressed in Ephesians 5:22, where it commands, "Husbands, love your wives, just as Christ loved the church and gave himself up for her to make her holy." Consequently, husbands need to wake up from their slumber and become pro-active, and exhibit behaviors that demonstrate love. There may have been many years of slumber, but now is the time to start.

When Harold came to see me for counseling, he was desperate to save his marriage. His wife told him she was thinking of leaving him for another man. She believed Harold did not know how to love her. She was doubtful that Harold could change, or that he would ever be capable of loving her. The basis of her conviction was the lack of love she had experienced in their *thirty plus year*s of marriage! Harold was a very hard worker. He ran a small family business throughout their marriage, but that business required an extreme amount of attention to maintain. As a result, Harold was figuratively asleep at the wheel regarding loving his wife. Beyond the shock of his wife's revelation was the reality that a recent widower from their church was proving to be a romantic rival. Having to suddenly compete for his wife's affections was quite unexpected for this man nearly sixty years of age. Like King Theoden, Harold awoke with a strong desire to do what he had not done in the past. He was the most motivated client I have ever had. At the start of counseling we dealt with Harold's understanding of the nature of love by defining what love is and what it is not.

For this second task, I will start with three mistaken ideas about love and then present four ideas in line with the concepts of love and respect as presented in the Bible.

Hard Work Does Not Equal Love

Men who love their wives actively provide for their family. The Bible says, "He who does not provide for his family is worse than an infidel," (1 Timothy 5:8, my paraphrase). Over the years, I have observed that when a husband complains about how much his wife spends on groceries, he probably has no clue of how to love his wife. Groceries are expensive, but he needs to love his wife enough to communicate about their food budget. The majority of men I have counseled understand the need for provision; unfortunately, they are so busy earning money that they don't demonstrate the kind of love their marriage requires.

Many husbands assume that enough material provision eliminates the need to contribute in other ways to their marriage. A very simplistic priority rubric might be as follows: First, love God; second, love your wife; third, work hard. If this rubric is close to correct, it is apparent that following the third command (work hard) is not a substitute for the second command (love wife). That was Harold's mistake. Is it yours?

Love Is Not Reciprocal

Men of Harold's generation were often guilty of confusing love with provision, while younger men often confuse love with reciprocity. Reciprocity is a fancy word that essentially means an equal exchange of goods, or more commonly, "If you scratch my back, I'll scratch yours." This kind of love is conditional. I love you as you love me. I'll earn a living if you watch the kids. If you put me through medical school, then I'll help you fulfill your career goals. Most crassly, I'll provide the money if you provide the sex.

This form of love can be very shallow, but it does provide the basis for many present marriages. Personal preferences are often elevated to the level of needs; these include financial success, attractiveness, thinness, domestic support, or recreational companionship. As long as needs are met, the marriage tends to work well. Since having our needs met is pleasurable, many marriage counselors focus on helping couples meet each other's needs. This approach is generally successful as long as the needs can be met or even negotiated.

Unfortunately, when needs can't or won't be met anymore, then divorce is usually not far behind. Not long ago, a famous politician left his wife after she came down with cancer. The divorce rate among couples with children who have significant physical disabilities approaches 90%. In a reciprocal arrangement, love is about the mutual meeting of needs, and when illness or the distraction of a child with a disability interferes, it is often "game over" for that marriage.

Expectations run very high when couples get married. This is normal. However, if expectations do not adjust to a realistic level, unhappiness will prevail. Marriage is not a ticket to having all our needs met. Reciprocity implies that if I do my part, then I will get what I want in return. There is a subtle deception to this common approach to marriage. The deception sounds like this, "If I provide *love* in terms of material provision, or in terms of affection, sex, domestic support, or companionship, and I patiently wait for my turn, then I will be rewarded. Unfortunately, life is not that fair.

Couples expect a 50/50 reciprocity. In reality, one person gets his or her needs met, but the other is unhappy with the return. Sometimes a person gets all he or she ever wanted and more. Since that feels good, that person selfishly wants even more. Good provision is no ultimate guarantee of a fair return on your efforts. Any return is uncertain. I may place a high priority on the attractiveness of my wife and our sex life, but circumstances beyond our control, such as physical illness may hinder our sexual activities. And all beauty eventually fades with age (Psalm 31:30). Love must be based on something beyond an exchange of goods.

Wives are not "starters" or "trophies." They are to be loved, even when nothing is returned in the exchange. Traditional marriage vows wisely recognize this reality. Marriage is promised to continue in "sickness and health" and whether "richer or poorer." This country's 50% divorce rate strongly suggests that an unacceptable exchange of "goods" trumps the marriage vow. Of course, not all divorces are traceable to unfulfilled expectations, but my counseling experience leads me to believe that this *is* a significant issue.

Hard evidence suggests that high expectations ruin marriages. Drs. Les and Leslie Parrott, the co-directors of the Center for Relationship Development at Seattle Pacific University, found through their research that certain "marriage myths" predict trouble for marriages. Such myths are directly related to expectations couples have about marital life. Some of those dangerous expectations could be categorized as follows: having similar desires (we will always be the same), life will always get better, the bad parts of life will be eliminated, and finally, marriage will meet all my psychological needs. Those findings, along with other factors that predict potential marital problems, are found in the Parrotts' popular book, *Saving Your Marriage Before it Starts*.[5] The second task in this guide involves moving away from a reciprocal meeting of needs as the definition of marital love and success.

Love Is Not Sentimentalism

Romance is an important part of a good marriage. If your wife's personality is inclined toward romance, than increasing the amount of romance will be a key to completing the task of showing love. Many passages in the Bible are quite romantic (see Song of Solomon). On the other hand, many couples confuse romance, which is good, with a belief that they must always feel "in love," which is dangerous. Sentimentalism is the demand for constant "feelings of love." This demand is simply unrealistic. Feelings will come and go in any marriage. Often there will be negative emotions, but love is not sentimentalism. Love is more than romance or feelings.

Surprisingly, many men are sentimentalists. While many women may enjoy the concept of romance and read romance novels, men often believe feelings should rule the day. I have a vivid memory of a couple I counseled where the husband said, "If marriage takes work, I don't want any part of it." By that statement he meant that marital love should just *flow*. He saw love only as a natural organic feeling. Working at feelings, in his mind, ruined the feelings. He was not interested in even reading books about marriage. In his mind, when feelings are lost, love has died. That particular client was a little extreme, but his beliefs are common. His wife was not so idealistic; she just wanted her husband to help discipline the kids and take her dancing now and again. He saw her demands as work. Why should he do what he didn't feel like doing? Doing the mundane did not fit with his definition of love as a sentimentalist.

Women are often longsuffering. If a woman believes love equals sentimentalism, she will often wait patiently, perhaps for years, for her husband to provide the feelings of love she seeks. Eventually, her own unrequited feelings are lost. When that happens she might bring her husband into counseling. At the beginning of their marriage counseling the wife announces, "I just don't love him anymore." That pronouncement means that we are at the red level of the marital destruction warning scale. Marriages that live by feelings are apt to die by them.

The indie movie, *500 Days of Summer,* tackles the notion of sentimentalism as experienced in contemporary relationships. The main character, Tom Hansen, falls "in love" with his co-worker, Summer. He interprets their relationship as true love. Summer, very unsentimentally, says she does not believe in true love. Later she leaves Tom when she does fall in love with someone else. He is the sentimentalist, and the movie portrays his feelings based love as being common, but immature. He tried to construct a love on feelings alone. Having lived by feelings, the movie shows him suffering in relation to those same feelings (he is rejected and depressed), but his suffering clears when he meets someone new. This illustrates that men base relationships on feelings as much as women do.

So what does love look like? What did I tell Harold? What is the slumbering king to do when he awakens with the goal of loving his wife? The following section describes the foundational elements of the task of showing love.

Love Has an Object

The book of Ephesians says husbands are to love their wives as Christ loved the church, and gave Himself up for her, making her spotless. A television automobile commercial talks about the relentless pursuit of perfection. This concept appeals to most men who understand that success takes hard work. The verse mentioned above calls men to the relentless pursuit of *her* perfection. It is not about me—it is all about the object. This is true romance—not a romance made of the passion of burning loins and bodice ripping, but a desire for the other's best. That best, should include all of the following: great sex, care for the other in illness, confrontation when needed, sharing, affection, spiritual betterment, and tons of help. That is the goal of the lover—to work for the best in the beloved.

In the 1970s and '80s, a respected professor dedicated himself to studying the nature of love. That man, Leo Buscaglia, a professor at the University of Southern California, began a course called "Love 101." It became one of the most popular college courses ever offered. One of Buscaglia's statements was, "Love is always bestowed as a gift—freely, willingly and without expectation. We don't love to be loved; we love to love."[6] How about you? Do you get up in the morning with the goal of bestowing love on your beloved? Do you have a vision of what would make your wife perfect, holy, happy, or better? Do you bestow love without thought of what you will get in return?

My pastor likes to state, "The Bible is a love story sandwiched between two marriages." The first marriage takes place in the Garden of Eden. The second marriage is the wedding feast in the book of Revelation. The Bible is all about how God would save His beloved. You can read the entirety of the Bible as a love story. Out of all the peoples of the world, he chose Israel to be his beloved nation. He bestowed love singularly on that nation. Israel then rejected God, pursing idols instead of the living God.

Idolatry is analogous to adultery in the Bible. In essence, the people of God continually ran from God to commit spiritual adultery. Israel's unfaithfulness is depicted in the book of Hosea. Hosea portrays God as a jilted lover. Throughout the Old Testament stories of the Bible, God used historical events, and the actions of surrounding nations, to variously save and discipline His people. Nothing actually worked to bring His people to Himself. So the Great Lover ultimately had to sacrifice His only Son. God sent Jesus in the flesh to save His special people, now known as His church. God sacrificed His only Son simply due to His great love. This was done so that all who believe might enjoy eternal bliss with God as originally experienced in the Garden of Eden. In fact, the Bible ends with a wedding feast, which ushers in the eternal marriage of Christ and His Bride (God's people). It's one big love story.

Christ's ultimate sacrifice models the fact that love will cost something personally. Time at the office and golf outings may need to be curtailed. Your own free time may wane while your wife pursues her interests; whatever activities are close to her heart. Money will be spent on vacations with your beloved. Places she would choose to go. It may seem like it will "kill you" to stay at the quaint bed and breakfast, but that is the kind of activity that may bring life back to your marriage.

God chooses us as His people, not because we are good or worthy, but because He is a loving king. He doesn't leave us because He is God. It is the same for earthly husbands. He loves his wife because he chooses to love. As much as it depends on him, he continues to love her. Love has an object—your wife.

Dr. Aramand Nicholi, a Harvard psychiatrist, notes that C.S. Lewis wrote that being in love leads one to desire the person apart from any need that person can meet, even the need for sexual gratification. Sexual desire is a fact about ourselves; it focuses on oneself, whereas being in love is about another, focused on the beloved. Dr. Nicholi quotes Lewis as stating, "Sexual desire...wants it, the thing in itself (sexual release, or person as object); being in love wants the Beloved (the person)."[7]

Love Is Spiritual

There is another conclusion we can draw from God's love story. Spiritual love is about modeling God's love and then responding to God's love by loving our wife. This removes the focus from how well my spouse is meeting my needs. Spiritual love is not about her, spiritual love is about God.

Many years ago, a wise Christian counselor was trying to describe the concepts of Christian marriage to couples in Kenya.

To accomplish this task, he came up with a drawing of a triangle where the husband and wife are placed at the base of the triangle across from one another. At the top of the triangle he placed God. The triangle illustration shows that as a couple gets closer to God, they get closer to one another.[8] A couple's level of intimacy is directly related to each member's level of spirituality. If the wife is real spiritual and the husband is not, then there is always some distance between them. There looms a possibility that a spouse might get "too spiritual." This creates unnatural distance; however, many husbands can grow spiritually and transform their marriages by completing the tasks in this book. Practically, the husband's spiritual growth might involve initiating church attendance, willingly attending church small groups, reading the Bible, or generally being more interested in his wife's spiritual life and promoting her spiritual growth. Ask her, "What can I do to be either more of a spiritual person or spiritual leader in our home?" Since love is spiritual, a secret avenue to a marriage transformation may simply come by way of personal spiritual growth.

Love is described well in 1 Corinithians13. It gives us the ultimate "honey do" list. Husbands need that. A couple came to see me many years ago. He worked as a mechanic for an auto dealership, where his work entailed completing a list of jobs that had been created by his service writer. He was comfortable with following a "to do" list. At home, he was often tired from his work, so he did little to help his wife domestically. Since his wife also worked all day, her definition of love meant helping out at home. She had in mind certain things he could do that would make a huge difference in their family life. So, we constructed a "honey do" list for him to perform when he got home (he usually got home about two hours sooner than his wife). He took to this concept well. As a result, when she arrived home, the things that made her life easier were done and then she could enjoy an evening with her husband. This caused her to feel loved. That was a simple matter.

Take a look at the following list from the aforementioned 1 Corinthians 13 and see where you need to work: "Love is patient, love is kind. It does not envy, it does not boast, it is not proud. It is not rude, it is not self-seeking, it is not easily angered, it keeps no record of wrongs. Love does not delight in evil but rejoices with the truth. It always protects, always trusts, always hopes, always perseveres. Love never fails."

Every husband will respond differently, but this list is God's definition of spiritual love. How are you doing with the patience, anger, self-seeking, or record keeping departments? Do you delight in evil, or do you truly want to protect your wife and see her grow more pure and holy than she is already? If you are as I once was, this list should transform your approach to marriage.

Note that the story of the auto mechanic and the list from the Bible are not exactly the same. The auto mechanic example was more about doing stuff, while the list from the Bible was about attitudes toward your wife. What they have in common is an active approach to marriage. You say you love your wife, so how do you demonstrate that love? A passive approach to loving your wife is no love at all. As Leo Buscaglia stated, "I have a very strong feeling that the opposite of love is not hate—it's apathy."[9]

Love Is Related to Gender

Men and women look at love differently. Notice some of the marriage titles on the bookstore shelf: *Men are from Mars, Women are from Venus; Men are like Waffles—Women are like Spaghetti*; and even, *Men are from Dirt, Women are from Men*. Gender differences are biblical. For marital love, God has different commands for each gender. Men must be commanded to love their wives, while women naturally love men. There is no direct command in the Bible for women to love their husbands because such a command is unnecessary. Instead, women are commanded to respect their husbands.

Women are given the command to respect or submit to their husbands because maintaining respect will require explicit faith from God. This is the area where women must trust God for their own transformation. Therefore, men must look to God for the faith required to love their wives, while wives must look to God for the faith to respect their husbands.[10]

Respect is easily lost in a marriage, but feelings of love (which are natural) die hard for many women. However, once those feeling are dead, they are hard to resuscitate. This explains some of the differences between men and women in terms of their approach to love. Since women naturally love, they sometimes make foolish choices. They "love" bad boys or tough guys because it is part of their nature to love. They may even choose a spouse they never respected from the beginning. Sometimes women believe they can change or convert their spouses. In time, without the building of respect, the wife's love also fades. If the husband does not discover he needs to "love his wife," the marriage will be troubled and loveless.

I don't believe that all marriages have to follow rigid gender patterns. Not all women are lovers seeking romance, and not all men are lugs who have to be commanded to love their wives. Yet, if the shoe fits, try it on. Ultimately, men and women tend to approach love differently. I coach the couples in my practice as follows: wives need to start every morning with the goal in mind, "I need to show my husband respect". However, husbands need to start every morning with this goal in mind, "I need to show love to my wife." Some marriages actually demonstrate gender role opposites.

The wife may be the breadwinner and have a leadership-oriented personality. She may possess the more dominate personality of the couple. They may both be pleased that the husband is the stay-at-home domestic caregiver. This in no way changes the spiritual requirement for him to be the prophet, priest, and king (spiritual leader) of his home. It does not eliminate his tasks of invitation, avoidance, and love. It may mean that reversing the curse of the fall will require him to demonstrate respect toward his wife as part of his love task. Whether showing love and respect or respect and love, the key point of this task is that love is being demonstrated in an effective manner.

Love Is Symbolic

This is perhaps the most transformative statement I can make about love. Women tend to see certain behaviors and attitudes as symbolic. This concept is a hard one for some men to wrap their minds around. Women often have expectations that are unique to them regarding how they define love. For instance, if a wife particularly values family time and evening meals together, then she will look for her husband to make being home on time for meals a priority. Other things that the husband may consider as important examples of love, such as flowers or phone calls during the day, may be meaningless to this particular woman. Another wife may simply want her husband to buy her flowers, while not caring when he arrives home or how often he calls.

The first wife sees the loving husband as one who fulfills a certain family role, the second wife sees the loving husband as one who does romantic things. A third wife may long for her husband to read the Bible with the family and fulfill a spiritual role. When the husband fulfills that particular behavior, it is symbolically read as an act of love. That symbolism is more important than any amount of money can buy.

Speaking of money, a financially sound couple came to see me for counseling. He worked a great deal and on his one day off would go into the backyard, unhitch his sport fishing boat, and head out into the Atlantic. He spent virtually no time with his wife and two daughters. His wife tearfully told me she wanted to get a divorce and find someone who would pay attention to their kids. The husband stated that she had never complained when he bought her a luxurious home, cars, a considerable wardrobe, and jewelry. I met with the husband twice and explained the fallacy of provision and the symbolic nature of love.

Two weeks later, the wife came to my office by herself. I expected the worst; however, her whole demeanor had changed. She joyfully recounted how on a weekday, her husband stayed home from the office, which he had never done before, came home, and invited her and his daughters to go to the mall. He took them shopping. Shopping was something he previously refused to do. He was determined to be the kind of husband his wife would love. In fact, she was beginning to find him irresistible, just like she did so many years ago.

It was the same success story with Harold. His wife did not want to leave him, but she wasn't feeling loved. Old dogs can learn new tricks. Affection, listening, communicating, planning retirement, and just spending time together spelled love for Harold's wife. He awoke from his slumber with a vengeance, and even though it was a late start—it wasn't too late. Harold quickly became an expert on all of those behaviors that spelled love for his wife.

How about you? What captures your attention to the point of neglecting your wife? King Theoden woke up in time to save his kingdom and the race of men. Is your kingdom dying for lack of demonstrable love? Do not wait for your wife to love you first. Bestow love freely without regard to return. Finally, make sure the love you give is the love she symbolically seeks.

Key Questions

1. Ask your wife if she thinks you are active or passive in bestowing love. Next, ask her if she thinks you give love to get something in return (i.e., are you nice just so she won't be mad, or so she will have sex with you, etc.), or do you give love unconditionally?
2. Next, ask her what behaviors or attitudes would be a symbolic gesture of love for her. Then make demonstrating that behavior or attitude an absolute priority in your life.
3. Remind yourself daily of your command, "Love your wife."

THE THIRD TASK:
Lead Your Wife

Somebody tell me, please, tell me if you can...What is the soul of man?

—Bruce Cockburn

What is a man? Nowadays you might be hard-pressed to respond with a quality definition. This question is especially difficult to answer in a postmodern society in which definitions are relative. The secular definition and consensus toward males often tends to be negative. I recently read an article in *The Chronicle of Higher Education* which said a secular college now offers a course to counter "discrimination" and negative stereotypes to which modern males are subjugated (kind of an anti-male bashing class). While such a course is probably excessive, the negative stereotypes abound.

Television often portrays men as impotent jerks (think Homer Simpson), perpetually immature (think Charlie Sheen), or as overly aggressive and dangerous (think of just about any Lifetime Channel movie). After all, men commit most violent crimes, and are seen as responsible for starting wars. How many times have you seen males portrayed as being unwilling to grow up or as someone who can't be trusted?

Somehow maleness in general is suspect. When a man asserts himself in marriage, the societal consensus is it would be better if the maleness were feminized. One hilarious scene from the movie *Heartbreak Ridge* portrays Clint Eastwood as a hard-bitten, cursing, old school marine drill sergeant who no longer fits the "new" feminized military. In an effort to win back his modern thinking ex-wife, the hardened sergeant sits outside a bar in his pickup truck secretly reading women's magazines, attempting to understand the feminine psyche. The entire movie mocks Clint Eastwood's macho image and how such men are emasculated in a feminine leaning society. However, these exact types of men are still needed in the event of war. Our society's messages related to masculinity are highly conflicted.

So how should a Christian man define himself? What is the soul of a man? What model should he follow in a faith-filled marriage? The biblical answer is that a man is to be "like Christ." Christ is our model in terms of spiritual life and practice, emotional health, and even in terms of what it means to be male.

Promise Keepers

In my marriage counseling practice a common complaint I often hear from wives is that her husband is not being a "spiritual leader." There is a sense among evangelical Christians that marriages require male leadership, and that the answer to the question, "What is man?" has something to do with spiritual leadership. The Promise Keeper's movement that was so strong in the 1990s gained much strength by focusing on this very theme.

Standing shoulder to shoulder with 50,000 other men in a domed stadium was unforgettable. It was also extremely loud. You could feel the vibration of the male bass voices singing upbeat choruses. It was more emotionally moving than I anticipated. Tears streamed down the face of the man who stood next to me as one of the speakers told us to re-visit past hurts. Another speaker told us to take our shoes off (ala Moses) so we could experience the cool stadium concrete in our socks while learning about submission to God.

I was touched by the admonitions to repent of racial discrimination and personal sin; moreover, I was attentive to what the speakers had to say about men. The model offered that weekend was one of service and the importance of following Jesus as servant leader. God gave His all on the cross for our sins; likewise, we should make sacrifices for our wives.

Another speaker preached forcefully on the concept of out-serving our wives even in the area of domestic duties. He acted out a mock fight with his wife in which they fought over who would iron the others' clothes, "That's my iron!" "No, that's my iron, I had it first!" The effect was inspiring, and many men who never helped their wives in the past went home and helped in new ways…at least for a while.

Since Jesus stooped to wash the feet of his disciples, we all could benefit from a little stooping. I need to show humility in front of my wife. Service and submission are part of the story, but perhaps an even bigger part was Christ's obedience to His Father. What is the soul of man? Sacrificial servant hood? Yes. Obedient follower of the heavenly Father to the extreme? Absolutely. Christ had a role to fulfill. He was always about His father's will, and we should be too.

Sacrificing self in the manner of Christ is a good place to start. This is discussed in detail in the second chapter of Philippians. Christ completed the sacrificial aspect of His role when He died to save us from our sins. We are to continue to model Christ's example of sacrifice and obedient service in marriage, however, the way we show that sacrificial love hopefully will not entail ultimate sacrifice (Christ already died as substitute for our sins). I would submit that there are other roles that Christ performed that we are also to model. When we fully model the various roles of Christ, we demonstrate a complete image of who we really are as men.

The Promise Keeper model views man as a servant leader. This model is supported by biblical examples of Christ's sacrifices for His beloved bride, the church. This model is part of what it means to be a man. Every man should be able to examine his life and answer the question, "How am I sacrificing my selfish desires for the sake of my beloved wife?" However, this model is only part of what the Bible intends as the model for man. If this is the only model, marriage would be more duty and drudgery than God ever intended. The next model of man is very different, and probably a reaction to the sacrifice model.

The Warrior Model

Several years ago I attended a Sunday school class hosted by church leaders eager to begin a men's ministry. We studied *Wild at Heart* by John Eldredge, who proposes that the soul of man is essentially wild in nature because God is also, in part, wild. Men, wounded by rejection or neglect from their earthly fathers, are taught by the church to repress their wilder natures and be "nice."

Eldredge suggests we model Christ by being "real men," and in a manner that is neither safe nor comfortable. He also suggests that purpose and meaning in life comes when a man realizes he has an enemy to fight (Satan), an adventure to live (placing God first), and a beauty to rescue (his wife).

Certainly, the antiseptic, ever-pleasing, never-offending, always approval seeking modern evangelical male leaves much to be desired. The modern model doesn't jive with the hard to swallow messages of Christ or with all those scruffy images in the Old Testament. While Christianity in its truest form has never been tame, the image of man as warrior, like Sampson, Joshua, or David is just one aspect of the total picture of the image of God. However, a theology of a free and wild God misses much of God's character both in terms of His tenderness and His sovereign consistency.

The soul of man in the image of God may indeed be wild, but Sampson and David were actually big losers in the relationship department. The Bible shows that sometimes wilder natures need further submission to a higher authority. As a psychologist, my own sense of the wild heart, back to nature, or warrior image is more supported by popular Jungian notions of personality (the anima and the animus, the shadow, the wolf, etc.), than the biblical model of Christ.

I asked my in-house expert on males—my wife—what she thought of the "wild man" idea. She agreed with Eldredge that deep down most women prefer a wild-man Christian over a wimp-man Christian. She also went on to observe with her usual acute insight that some women would prefer a relationship in which they control the man. Many men are comfortable with passivity. Is the pacifist man somehow outside the biblical ballpark? Is the choice only between warrior and pacifist? What about the servant leader? The answer is that there are multiple roles for Christian husbands to fulfill.

The warrior view makes a valid point that being a good Christian male is often a wild adventure and may have nothing to do with being nice. For example, a manly Christian lawyer in my town once led a protest against pornographers in our town. He faced off against the owners of adult bookstores, which led to their banishment from the community. He wasn't very nice and it was more of a wild ride than a pretty sight. And so it goes in marriage, which may require both tough mindedness and wildness in varying degrees. Ultimately, the warrior image, like the servant image is not all there is to the picture God gives us in the Bible. Life takes on new meaning when men realize they have some exciting roles to fulfill by faith in marriage.

Our View of God

A person's view of man tends to follow his or her view of God. For instance, if a man views God the Father as harsh and unforgiving, he may act in a similar vein by harshly giving orders to his wife and kids. A man who views God as loving and forgiving will treat his family likewise. A correct view of God should get us closer to how a man should live. It is interesting then to consider whether we possess an appropriate image of God.

When I speak about the image of God in groups, I perform the following exercise. I pass out 3X5 cards and ask the men in the audience to list up to three, one word descriptors for God. The answers I often receive include master, gracious, righteous, awesome, love, judge, leader, etc. Wild and servant are rarely mentioned. My answer is three descriptors found in the Bible: holy, holy, holy. While there are many correct answers to this exercise, my question is, "Which view of God will lead us to a correct view of who we should be as men?" I believe the next view of God has the ability to completely transform our marriages.

Prophet, Priest, and King

The idea of being a sacrificial servant or wild warrior may seem radical, but biblical reality usually is radical. When the first Adam failed, our first model went out the window. The last Adam, Jesus Christ, is a perfect model; therefore, our standard, mold, and forerunner. God is defined by his Son, Jesus Christ. The definition of man that we see in Jesus is radical, and given this radical nature, is a model of manhood that can *only* be accepted by faith. In defining manhood and becoming like Christ, the need to depend on the Holy Spirit and act in faith is even greater. So, what does the model of Christ look like?

The Bible gives positive and negative examples for most of the important lessons it teaches. For example, in Proverbs, we see examples of the blessings of the wise (the carrot, if you will), and also the negative consequences that befall the unwise (the stick). Would God leave the question, "What are the key characteristics of a man?" out of the Bible? Not a chance. The Old Testament is filled with stories of prophets, priests, and kings. These are all types of Christ in either the positive or negative sense. The good kings point to, or model, a type of the good King Jesus to come. The bad kings are not like Jesus to come. They are set as negative examples.

Learning by negative example is a great teaching technique. When I used to go rock climbing, I read mountain climbing bulletins describing rock climbing disasters. By reading them, I saw stupid mistakes others made (i.e. some climbers didn't bring warm clothing so they froze to death; some didn't bring a long enough rope when they repelled down, etc.) and I learned how to proceed in a safe manner. Readers of the magazine *Flying*, know that it contains a popular column on pilot error to teach about better and safe piloting. Likewise, the Bible provides stories of prophets, priests, and kings from whom we may learn how to be the heads of our homes in both positive and negative ways. Not everything King David did was good; very little of what Samson did was good.

As a young man, I listened with intent to the stories of the kings of the Old Testament as they battled or led in certain ways. I longed to live during the Old Testament era because if I had been there I know I would have been a good king (at least in my mind). Barring time travel, there seemed to be no relationship to the present. But I have since discovered that the command to model Christ in my marriage applies to the images and types of Christ in the stories of the Old Testament. So what should it look like for me to be the prophet, priest, and king of my home?

All true prophets spoke the exact words that God spoke to them. They foretold or spoke forth the Word of God. A modern prophet speaks the Word of God to his wife and family. Being a prophet means having regular times of family devotions where the Word of God is read to or with our wife or children. The reading of the Word of God out loud is a simple way for a husband to be a prophet in his home.

The next aspect of biblical maleness is the role of priest. In the Old Testament, the high priest entered the Holy of Holies to make sacrifices for the people once a year. The book of Hebrews tells us that Christ completed the sacrifices, but He still intercedes for His people to this day. He prays for us. He prays for His bride. To be like Christ, we should pray daily for our wives and children. Before Job faced his tribulation, he was the most righteous and blessed man on earth. Job's very existence irked Satan. One of the reasons he got under Satan's skin is he prayed daily for his children lest any of them might sin against God. His concern was one of holiness. It should be your concern as well.

As kings of our homes, it is important to note that all kings of biblical history led—it's just the direction of their leadership that differed. Some were good and some were evil. The servant leader is still an important theme. "Lording over our wives," is never right, and in fact, sinful.

For years I told my married male clients they are like CEOs of a large company. Most white-collar men fantasize about how they would run the company if they were in charge. Now they see they are already in charge of something with eternal significance. Those who shift priority from running a business to running a marriage receive a blessing in this life and the next.

We are accountable in terms of what kind of prophet, priest, and king we are on earth. The fulfillment of these may go a long way in marking the basis of eternal rewards and judgments. If I am a king, I ought to live and act accordingly. A quick review of 1 and 2 Kings in the Old Testament makes for a good self-study to look for examples. Forty kings are recorded and each story is presented in a similar format; so-in-so led (note, they all led) the people of Israel. Then the king is either pronounced good or bad. Take a look for yourself and assess the actions of each king. Most are bad, and most committed the same error—idol worship with a heavy dose of sexual immorality.

These same issues plague men today. Read Revelation 2:12-17. This letter to the church at Pergamos sounds like it is written just for today. This is a church that lives in an area where Satan is on the throne, and that church is in a compromising position before God. The church is chided for getting involved in idolatry with a heavy dose of sexual immorality. Sound familiar? The same issue for the kings of the Old Testament, the same issue for the church at Pergamos, is the same issue for us as kings in our marriages.

Will we lead our family to worship God, or will we lead them toward idolatry and sexual immorality? As we previously read in Revelation 2:17 states that those who persevere in this specific area will be given a white stone engraved with a new name that only God and the holder will know. The man who leads in the right direction, despite idolatry and sexual immorality, gets a "secret" name. Interestingly, the stone is white, indicative of sexual purity.

The roles of prophet, priest, and king have a spiritual nature, so they can only be accomplished by faith. We have to trust fully in our Heavenly Father in order to fulfill these roles. One more reminder, these roles have nothing to dominating our wife and our children, but as a spiritual task these roles involve submission to our King.

Practical Suggestions

Leadership is task number three. We often make things more complicated than they need to be. Here are some practical suggestions for leading your family:

1. **Have a regular time of Bible reading.** Be consistent and stick to it just like you would a personal training schedule. It is surprising how little time contemporary Christians spend reading the Bible. If you are new to Bible reading, start by simply reading a chapter a day in the book of Proverbs in the Old Testament and/or the book of John in the New Testament. Proverbs provides wisdom for living, and the book of John teaches about Jesus Christ. When your wife or children see you reading the Bible, you will be setting an important leadership example. Realize you do not have to make anyone else read the Bible. A leader simply sets the example. If your wife likes the idea, read her passages to her at bedtime. Former President Jimmy Carter and his wife Roslyn have spent every night of their long married life taking turns reading aloud one chapter of the Bible every night. They also rotate reading the chapters in English and Spanish to maintain their Spanish language

skills. When Jimmy is away on a peace mission, they still read the same chapter while apart.

2. **Have a consistent time when you pray for yourself, your marriage, and your children.** Pray for them by name, and if you are familiar with Bible passages, use those when you pray. If you are not familiar with Bible passages, then begin practical suggestion number one above and begin to find Bible verses you would like to use in your prayers. There is no right or wrong verses to recite while praying. Offer to pray out loud before dinner and when you go to bed at night—even if you have never prayed out loud before. These prayers can be very simple; thanking God for His providing food and taking care of you throughout the day, and then asking for His help wherever it is needed. The husband should lead in prayer. This is an important aspect of leadership task number three, so do not delegate this job to someone else. This is a husband's role as family priest. Of course, your wife can pray, also. (I am not being spiritually sexist here. In fact, women may lead their homes in prayer, however the point of this book is to involve men in the six tasks of marital transformation. Leading in prayer, by definition creates male spiritual leadership in the home.)

3. **Get your family to church.** This aspect of leadership task number three could be the aspect that most transforms your marriage and reverses the curse under which you are living. Many times in contemporary Christian homes when the marriage is not going well, church attendance drops off. This is where male spiritual leadership can have the greatest impact. Think of barriers to church attendance and mentally problem-solve them. Do not have a church home? Pick one that preaches from the Bible and just start attending. Ask for your wife's input and if she has opinion as to which church she likes best, try it first. Ask her what would help get her out the door. Some common practical issues might include; help getting the kids ready (do this gladly), helping her get up on Sunday morning by not

keeping her up late on Saturday night, completing household tasks if she is going to take time to go church (offer to do them), and finally, she may be concerned about how the kids will behave and whether the nursery services are adequate (you can simply relieve her of those responsibilities when you get to church). Sitting in church, meeting other Christians, receiving good teaching, and generally worshipping God together could be a real game changer. When I was a kid, there was an ad campaign that declared, "The family that prays together, stays together." I have seen this to be true, so get to work on leading your family to church.

Key Questions

1. Which marriage model is new to your mind and how would you assess it?
    a. The modern "sensitive" male—the pacifist type.
    b. The servant leader with an emphasis on serving both in the church and in the home.
    c. The "wild-man" theory—the slightly dangerous male.
    d. The prophet, priest, and king model.

2. Which model are you presently closest to following right now? What would it look like if you started to the follow the prophet, priest and king model?

3. Review the above questions and answers with your wife. Does she agree? Discuss how she would feel if you started to lead your family as a prophet, priest and king.

THE FOURTH TASK:
Avoid Temptation

There is a point in every "lifeboat" movie where one of the survivors starts going crazy and drinking the salty sea water. Everyone else in the raft screams for him not to do it, but he just can't stop himself. Lust is like that. You just keep drinking the sea water and wanting more no matter that it is making you sick and thirstier than when you started. A man under the spell of lust would drink the whole ocean...

—Don McCulloch (based on an idea from statements made by Dr. Mark Laaser founder of Faithful and True Ministries)

The problem with sexuality is that it is oversold. We want it to provide satisfaction beyond God's original intent. Sex is indeed the glue that binds a marriage. However, sex cannot bind a troubled relationship, any more than Erector Set pieces can serve as rivets for a jet liner.

Sex sells. It sells just about everything these days. Unless you cut yourself off from the internet, television, magazines, and even billboards you see products purposively paired with sexuality. That is for one simple reason. God created the sight of female nudity as something men don't tend to miss. Advertising executives use this reality to grab your attention and sell their products. Let's call this the "Madison Avenue" approach.

Of course, our wives suffer the most from comparisons to Madison Avenue images. They can never measure up because these images are not real. A recent newspaper article[11] described how country singer Faith Hill's appearance on the cover of *Redbook* magazine had been doctored. Faith Hill is an attractive woman, but for the magazine cover her beauty was "further enhanced." This included making her waist appear impossibly small, giving her a new (thinner) arm, and ridding her any of other human qualities such as crow's feet, neck lines, and even "back fat." When Madison Avenue continually portrays women with inhuman qualities and features (no flaws and no fat allowed) it is no wonder that women suffer self-image problems.

Husbands have a large role to play in modeling the acceptance of Christ and re-assuring their wives of their God-given beauty. The reason some wives are not "into sex" as they get older is they have been made to feel too ugly by Madison Avenue and perhaps even their husband's behavior. A husband who accepts Madison Avenue's version of beauty subtlety conveys to his wife that she is not physically attractive. Madison Avenue and the fashion industry have successfully brainwashed a generation of women into believing their bodies are not good enough, even though God created them all good.

Consider the recent fashion trend which one female critic called "womb wear" (low-slung pants and short tops that continually expose the area well below the female belly button). This style can only fit the young. Previous fashions trends exploited either legs or breasts and were more in keeping with classic beauty. The present standard only glorifies youth and waistlines that befit women who have never had a child. This fashion sexualizes teens and pre-teens, and blatantly de-sexualizes any women with a normal waistline. As result, Faith Hill, who possesses classic beauty, had to have her waistline reduced before she appeared on a magazine cover.

Unrealistic and sexual image bombardment brings major consequences. Men begin to see women as objects and/or products rather than human beings. They mentally rate women according to the standards created by Madison Avenue. They begin to expect their wives to dress and act in certain sexual ways (as seen on TV!). A creeping but profound dissatisfaction takes over, along with a sense that sex with their wife is no longer fulfilling.

If men view pornography (which is even more detached from reality) the problem is only made worse. A secular university studied the effects of pornography and concluded that it made men less happy with their partners (rather than creating a sexual zip in their relationship). Sexual overexposure in our society has a strong subliminal effect that tends to kill sexual intimacy over time, like a slow growing cancer.

All men are susceptible to the sexual spell cast by our market-driven society. Men begin to evaluate women simply in terms of their bodies. I thought I was above this; not that I didn't notice women's bodies, but I didn't believe I was paying that much attention.

In South Florida, where I reside, women quite often wear very little in the hot climate. I would have denied this exposure was having any personal impact on how I looked at women, until I took a trip overseas with a conservative religious group. The climate at our destination was even hotter than South Florida, so we were all happy to swim in the afternoons at a local public pool. All the women on the trip wore modest one-piece bathing suits. By our second day, I became aware of something I am ashamed to admit. I was looking directly into the eyes of all the women with whom I was conversing at the pool. Their attire was not asking me to notice their bodies. Instead, I noticed details and beauty in their faces. It made me realize that I don't tend to notice women's faces as much as I should.

This change reminded me of life in the cold Midwest, where I would notice the beauty of the faces of well-bundled women in winter time. I had been conditioned to automatically notice and evaluate women in terms of the Madison Avenue image. This was an important revelation. Insight is the beginning of changing the process of how we view anything, including the opposite sex. Women in general, and our wives in particular, are not sex objects. Now I make a concerted effort to look women in the eyes when I speak with them. (Yes, my wife had already suggested this strategy to me, long before I took that trip.)

Men are always going to notice women. And a woman who dresses to be noticed will not be ignored. Men are sexual creatures, and that is how God made us. Most women are either naïve to this fact or they make use of it to gain male attention. In one psychological study[12], the amount of male sex hormones (testosterone levels) in the blood stream were measured as male college students went about their day. There was a significant rise in testosterone levels whenever males simply stood next to females and especially when they conversed. Men are made to respond sexually to women. Imagine what happens in more provocative settings than just chatting in a college classroom!

Men are more aroused sexually by visual stimulation than are women; men are much more visually oriented. The visual fields in the back of the eyes (consisting of what are called rods and cones) are different for men and women. Men rely more on cones, the color sensors, in the center of the visual fields where there is also more detail. Men in general notice color and image detail more than women.

Women rely more on the rods on the periphery of the visual fields. Rods are light sensitive, and not color sensitive, this means that women see better in the dark. Hence, a woman is a better driver at night, and a man will be more sensitive to the subtle differences in whether an item of clothing is modest or immodest. Just ask any responsible father of a teenage daughter. He sees what other men see, and he asks his daughter to rethink her wardrobe selection even though she may honestly not see a problem.

The combination of elevations in testosterone levels and visual stimulation sensitivity makes men prime targets for pornography consumption. In the face of arousing sexual images, adrenaline is also pumped into the bloodstream creating quite a physiological rush. This adrenaline rush has two effects. First, images viewed under arousal tend to get stamped into our brain's memory banks. In other words, pornographic images tend to stay with males (much like a soldier's mental images from adrenaline fueled combat tend to stick with him). Second, in some men, the rush brought about in viewing pornography can cause physiological proclivity to addiction. More graphic images are sought in an effort to re-create those rush feelings. Eventually, there is a gradual numbness toward normal sex. Pornography, rather than stimulating greater sexuality, actually is marital sex's executioner.

In the introduction to this book, I stated men get angry and women get depressed. I might as well have said men use pornography to deal with their emotions (especially un-resolved anger) and women end up depressed by their husband's abandonment to the fantasy world on the internet.

Dr. Mary Ann Layden, co-director of the sexual trauma and psychopathology program at the University of Pennsylvania, testified before the U. S. Senate on November 18, 2004:

> Pornography, by its very nature, is an equal opportunity toxin. It damages the viewer, the performer, and the spouses and the children of the viewers and the performers...My clinical experience indicates that the spouses of porn viewers are often depressed, and are more likely to have eating disorders, body image disorders and low self-esteem. These wives can't function in the fake sexual world in which their husbands live. The wives may try to please their spouse by engaging in sexual behaviors that they find degrading.[13]

Years ago, a young married woman came to me for marriage counseling. She was depressed. She wanted advice regarding her husband. He had converted their garage into a movie studio and would lock himself in that garage every night (away from her and their children) so he could watch pornography in private. He had essentially left his family for pornography. I could do little to help this sad woman because her husband had no intentions of seeing me or seeking help. This story made a big impression on me, because at the time it was such an exception. The internet has changed that. Now many husbands leave their wives nightly for pornographic images. Wives are depressed and husbands are not feeling much better. Sex cannot provide beyond what God intended it to provide. Erector set rivets won't hold a jet liner together. Balance is desperately needed.

The fourth task of a contemporary Christian marriage is to avoid temptation. Reversing the curse on marriage means not only leading and inviting your wife to marriage transformation and showing unconditional love, but it also requires balance by avoiding pornography and sexual imbalance. The task of avoidance can best be accomplished by adhering to the following corrective principles.

Corrective Principle #1: Avoid Behavior to Which There Is No End

A common theme among men who struggle with sexual balance is an obsession with behavior that is seemingly unending. Let me give an example. I love parties, but I would not like to go to a party that never ends—no matter how lovely the setting, hosts, and guests. The constant search for the party life is shallow and immature. Money is a wonderful thing, but the endless pursuit of money is vanity. Every male is commanded to work, but nonstop work is drudgery.

The pursuit of sexual pleasure in and of itself is an endless and ultimately deadening toil. God had Solomon explore all these options in the book of Ecclesiastes. Solomon concluded for our benefit that the endless pursuit of physical and aesthetic pleasures is vanity.

Practical Suggestions

Don't click on any internet sites that involve sexual content (even if it is just written content), because it will never end. Don't stare at attractive women. Not that you cannot notice their beauty, but staring has no end. Moreover, staring is rude and doesn't respect your spouse. Don't create unholy sexual fantasies in your mind, because that practice never ends. Avoid behaviors that have no end.

God made men with eternity in their hearts, and they long for intimacy with the living God. Endless pursuit of sexual pleasure is no filler for a real encounter with the eternal God. Ask yourself, before you look on the internet, create images in your mind, or stare a hole through a woman, "Will this behavior have a satisfying end?" If the answer is no, then avoid that behavior. If you are addicted to pornography, then see the resources and suggestions I have in the appendix for this chapter.

Corrective Principle #2: Fast from Sexual Stimulation

If your hormones are working on overdrive from all the sexual stimulation that you have allowed in your life, your system needs a rest. If you have been involved with pornography at all, then you are out of balance and need to reset your sexual thermostat. Fast from all the sexual stimulation you can reasonably control. Turn off the television at night for several months. Avoid the internet. Find some accountability. And set your computer so that any sites with sexual content (even so-called mild stuff) is blocked or filtered. Toss the material from under your bed or anything else that is used for sexual stimulation.

Sexual fasting involves refraining from sex, but it also has a specific purpose; to re-set your sexual thermostat and devote time to praying to God. This should be discussed with your wife so she will not feel rejected. I would pick a period of time that you can mutually agree upon. This could be a matter of weeks to a couple of months. The urges to look at racy imagines on television or online when those outlets are not available will cause you to begin an on-going conversation with the living God. Sexual fasting combined with prayer is the way to find balance. Ask for God's forgiveness. Use that prayer time to ask the Lord to begin to appreciate your wife's body. Begin to allow your mind to cultivate a desire for her and not for the images brought to you via Madison Avenue or elsewhere. Of course, the fasting will need to come to an end, and with it will come a newfound appreciation of your wife's body.

Practical Suggestions

Frequent sex with your wife is a good antidote for living in a sexually saturated culture. In fact, the apostle Paul (I Corinthians 7:5), says husbands and wives should not deny each other access to their bodies. It is actually sinful for a husband to let his emotions keep him from meeting the sexual needs of his wife. It is sinful for couples to withhold or avoid each other sexually within marriage because it leads to temptation to sexual activity outside marriage. On a practical level, sexuality can be drab and routine if the purpose of sexuality is only a release valve. For that reason, and others, there are times to abstain from sex (and not seek sexual stimulation elsewhere). During that time you can pray and your desire for your wife's body will properly increase. When the sexual fasting is over, you can both enjoy fresh sexual intimacy. A healthy sex life will have a natural ebb and flow. It will not be "sky rockets in flight" every night.

Corrective Principle #3: Reverse the Curse on Your Sex Life

If sexual intimacy is problematic due to avoidance, unrealistic expectations, or unholy behavior (pornographic influence), then you need to reverse the curse in your marriage. This is accomplished by developing a biblical approach to sexuality.

The Bible is never prudish regarding sexuality. God created sexuality and he expects married couples to engage in sexual activity frequently for both pleasure and procreation. While the book of Ecclesiastes, mentioned above, warns against the lack of fulfillment in the endless pursuit of sexuality for its own end, Solomon in no way denies that sexuality is pleasurable. The Song of Solomon is a detailed celebration of sexuality within a marriage. My clients often do not realize that a complete book of the Bible is dedicated to sexual intimacy.

Biblical sexuality does set boundaries—all forms of non-marital sexuality are sanctioned against one way or another. This includes, but is not limited to adultery, sex between singles, sex between members of the same gender, incest, and bestiality. Sodomy is especially ruled out due to its association with the previous list. The above behaviors are the staple content of pornography, so pornography is out of bounds on both psychological and biblical grounds. Masturbation is not on the list as it is not dealt with directly in Bible. Masturbation should be viewed in context of what has already been stated in this chapter. Masturbation connected to lust and pornography will eventually harm the intimacy of our marriages. It should be kept in mind that our wives bodies are to be the focus of any sexual thought or activities. The focus on masturbation is often selfish sexual pleasure making it counterproductive to mutual sexual fulfillment.

In reversing the curse, behavior prior to the fall of man is instructive. In fact, the verse right before the fall of man, which is Genesis 2:25 says, "And they were both naked, the man and his wife, and were not ashamed." Prior to the curse, Adam and Eve, reveled, enjoyed, accessed, and fully explored each other's nakedness. There was no shame or holding back. They were intimate in every sense of the word. Notice that it specifically says that it was "the man and his wife." This is a tip that this level of intimacy is not meant for a crowd, relatives, non-married couples, or Madison Avenue. Sexual intimacy is a private matter.

Adam and Eve were in paradise! Later, the naked body of the beloved is extolled in the Song of Solomon. And after the coming of Jesus, Paul tells us, the husband's body belongs to the woman, and the woman's body belongs to the man (see I Corinthians 7:2 – 5). Biblical sexuality celebrates the naked body of the spouse.

A special admonition is given in Proverbs 5:18-19, which says, "Let your fountain be blessed, and rejoice in the wife of your youth, as a loving deer and a graceful doe, let her breasts satisfy you at all times; and always be enraptured with her love." Note it is the wife of your youth's breasts that are to be your focus. Transformed intimacy begins with letting your wife's breasts and her lovemaking be your total source of sexual fulfillment.

Practical Suggestion

Let your wife's body, unadorned as was Eve's before the fall, become your focus. Spend time naked in each other's presence. This may not be easy for either of you at first. Again, many women are not comfortable with their bodies because of Madison Avenue or a husband's prior insensitivity. Make sure you have her permission and go slowly with this suggestion, but try to make her body the focus of your lovemaking. In addition to visual exploration, which may be threatening, begin with gentle touch or massage. Ultimately, it is your wife's body that you want to have in the forefront of your mind.

What if you already have a fairly balanced view of sexuality? What if you are already avoiding the messages of Madison Avenue or pornography? What if your wife is comfortable with her body? What are some ideas that may transform intimacy?

Transformative Principle #1: Keep Intimacy Simple and Sacred (K.I.S.S.)

In a sense, the Bible encourages us to K.I.S.S. our wives. This begins with letting our wife's body enrapture and thrill us. If sexual fulfillment requires a whole lot of props, settings, and standards, it is probably not what the Bible intended. For example, if a husband is not turned on unless his wife wears something specific, or performs in some specific way, things have gotten out of balance. The Bible is not opposed to dressing, smelling, or acting in a sensual manner, but if the thrill of your wife's breasts are lost, things are no longer simple.

Some requests by husbands, fueled by pornography or our pornographic culture, are not sacred. We should seek increase in our wife's sense of holiness even in our sexuality. She should never be encouraged to do something for which she is uncomfortable. If she is not completely comfortable, then the marriage bed is no longer sacred.

This is not dull sexuality, but it is productive sexuality. Sexuality was created for some obvious purposes. One productive purpose is to have children. The Bible encourages married couples to have children, saying it is a great blessing. The whole process, except for the pain of childbirth (which was affected by the curse) is to be celebrated. The second productive purpose for sexuality is to bind couples—the Bible talks of "two becoming one." Sexual intimacy should productively increase psychological intimacy. A third productive purpose for sexuality is pleasure for both partners.

A simple approach to sexuality often produces intense pleasure because it not about the peripherals—it about enjoying each other's bodies. When a wife feels the focus is on her, and nothing unholy is going to occur, then she can feel safe and free to fully enjoy sexual intimacy. Sex is a pleasure in such an environment and the command to have frequent sex is no chore.

Several years back, researchers at the University of Chicago conducted a study of sexuality that is considered to be one of the more accurate surveys in recent times. Hidden in the results, not widely publicized, was the following gem: Married women who regularly attended church were in the category of female respondents reporting the greatest number of orgasms over all other categories.[14] That is productive sexuality for pleasure! Just what God intended. The magazines at the checkout counter may offer all kinds of "new" sexual advice, but ultimately couples who make sexuality simple and sacred are having the most pleasure.

Speaking of pleasure, the Song of Solomon does give some hints at what makes for excellent lovemaking. Read this book on your own, or better yet, read it to your wife. Notice that the sensuality of the spoken word and poetry is part of sexual intimacy. Notice and even mark those different passages that unleash and celebrate all of the lovers' senses: hearing, sight, touch, smell, and even taste.

Transformative Principle #2: Don't Be So Selfish

Some men approach sexuality and lovemaking only in terms of their needs. A spiritual secret is that Christians should think of others before they think of themselves. While this is a general truism, it applies very well to our sex lives. Since a husband is commanded to love his wife, he should ask his wife what she would enjoy and then enjoy that behavior along with her. Focus on meeting her sexual needs consistently and if she is not selfish, she will probably reciprocate with the actions you find most pleasing. Perhaps you have been married a while and still don't know what would actually be enjoyable for your spouse. Ask her and then invite her to participate in that for which she has been longing. Transformed intimacy can be dramatic!

Not approaching your wife and inviting her to engage in sexual intimacy is a common way of being selfish. Don't let the initiation of sexual intimacy rest on her shoulders. Like you, she probably already has a lot on her shoulders. Take the lead in inviting her to the type of sexual intimacy she would most like to experience. Along those lines, a woman's body is governed by monthly cycles, so she will be more open to sexual intimacy on some days more than others. The unselfish husband should be aware of her cycle, and adjust his own expectations in accordance with that cycle. This awareness will require communication.

Sometimes there are instances when simple touching and affection should be the main summation of lovemaking. When a wife knows she doesn't always have to have sex, she may be relieved. In turn, if sexual intimacy is regularly initiated by the husband, he will be sure to have his needs met, as well. Transformed sexuality will follow a natural cycle that is optimally satisfying. The beginning of this chapter stated we cannot make sex become more than it was ever intended to be, but unselfish sex is quite fulfilling.

The possibility of rejection and need for communication means that transformed intimacy takes some deliberate work on the part of the husband. A selfish and perhaps lazy approach to sexuality is to "just let it happen." This means that the wife ends up with the responsibility for sexual intimacy. A pro-active unselfish approach by the husband orchestrates the opportunity for transformed sexuality.

Transformative Principle #3: Be the Prophet, Priest, and King of Your Sex Life

In the earlier chapter on the man's roles in the marriage of prophet, priest, and king, we noted that kings of the Old Testament were either leading toward or leading away from idolatry. So it is in your home, even, and maybe especially, when it comes to your sex life.

A good prophet speaks the word of God. This includes the passages in the Bible that clearly show that sex is good, marital nakedness is good, and her breasts are satisfying. As priest, the husband should initiate the reading of the Song of Solomon and any other appropriate passages on love and sexuality. God does speak through various types of written word. Many men have found that the reading of uplifting poetry is a wonderful addition to romancing your wife. Even better, write your own poetry.

The prophet tells his wife how satisfying her body is to him, even when natural changes occur due to age. A prophet celebrates the physical assets she possesses. A prophet doesn't act like a martyr, nor is he smug about his acceptance of his wife's non-airbrushed appearance. Proper spiritual leadership is a big turn-on for many women. Fulfilling your role as prophet makes you more physically attractive to your wife.   The priest seeks the holiness of his wife. To do so, he prays to not be unduly influenced by the world. Similarly, the husband needs the wife's prayers of protection in this area. The husband needs to get over the idea that his wife's holiness is the death knell to their sex life. Great sex is a simple and sacred pleasure. The world is selling you a lie if you think it has to be something else.

A good king in the Old Testament had to go against the grain to clean up the sexual climate of his nation. So it is with the spiritual kings of our homes. Are we leading our families toward or away from society's current pornographic culture? There really is only one way or the other. A good leader seeks to create a holy environment for his family, knowing that environment is the best environment for his wife and children.

The king, as the spiritual head of the home, is the one who is the arbiter of loveliness. His blessing and sanctioning of his wife's beauty bestows good self-esteem and body image in his wife. If his wife feels ugly, the husband's job is to bring her up by both his words and deeds. In today's society, she needs his constant blessing in this area. A husband cannot turn a blind eye to this responsibility, because in most cases, the wife is being told something negative by Madison Avenue on a daily basis.

Key Questions

Find some uninterrupted time alone with your wife. Perhaps at a park or other relaxing setting and then ask her the following questions:

1. To what extent do you think I evaluate you and other women by Madison Avenue standards?
2. Would you be more comfortable if I spent less time on the computer, watching certain shows on TV, or less time on the golf course? What amount of time on these activities would make you comfortable?
3. Do I spend too much time on Facebook or social media?
4. Do you think I have an unbalanced or pornographic approach to our sexual intimacy? Do you think our sexual intimacy is simple and sacred?
5. What are some of the barriers that make having sex a chore? Is there any one thing I can change or help you with that will making having sex easier for you?
6. How specifically can I be more unselfish in our lovemaking? What is something you have dreamed of happening in our sex life but never shared with me because you did not believe I would make it happen?

THE FIFTH TASK:
Nurture Significance

Many Christians...find themselves defeated by the most psychological weapon that Satan uses against them. This weapon has the effectiveness of a deadly missile. Its name? Low self-esteem. Satan's greatest psychological weapon is a gut level feeling of inferiority, inadequacy, and low self-worth. This feeling shackles many Christians, in spite of wonderful spiritual experiences and knowledge of God's Word. Although they understand their position as sons and daughters of God, they are tied up in knots, bound by a terrible feeling of inferiority, and chained to a deep sense of worthlessness.
—David A. Seamands, *Healing For Damaged Emotions*

I admit it. Even though I am a psychologist, I used to pooh-pooh the importance of self-esteem in the lives of my clients. Why? One snobbish reason is that psychologists in general often have trouble with the "unscientific" nature of the concept. Self-esteem is a hard concept to measure accurately.

Secondly, as a Christian, the emphasis on "the self" in self-esteem sends all kinds of red flags for my conservative sensibilities. Is it really spiritual to be so concerned about ourselves? Certainly modern culture has gone way over the top in this emphasis. Just check out the titles on the magazines at the grocery checkout counter.

Third, I just wasn't sure how more talk about self—in a pop psychology sort of way—would actually help anyone. I was wrong in terms of human reasoning, biblically, and as a husband.

On a human level, self-esteem is a popular topic because it reflects a real concern in the lives of individuals. Take an example from my private practice. Rarely do I see clients whom I know personally. It's not considered a good idea, yet when a respected member of my church basically demanded to see me, I relented. I felt smug to be consulted, but I soon realized he had his own agenda. He wanted us to study a self-help book about self-esteem which he had selected. Again I resisted (I'm a difficult person), but in the end we studied his book. The outcome? A mature Christian was helped by a self-help, self-esteem book. I then started using some of the material with my clients.

Another client was studying to become a respiratory therapist when he came to see me. He had a fear of needles, to the point of fainting. This was not a good trait in a profession cluttered with bodily fluids and IV lines. I told him I thought I could help him through some routine behavioral techniques. As the sessions progressed, he talked more about his unhappy marriage and some other uncontrollable negative events in his life than his initial problem. His faith was virtually non-existent. I felt compelled to give him the book, *Believe in the God who Believes in You*, by Robert Schuller[15]. I don't use Schuller's books in my practice, and I don't even know why I was prompted to suggest that book, which is basically a feel-good, God loves you sort of self-esteem book. However, I purchased it and gave it to him. He read it, and his faith and self-esteem improved greatly. His fear of needles went away, and he was much more hopeful about his relationships when he stopped seeing me. His was a success story for improving self-esteem, as well as faith.

A few years later, I was offered a job to be the supervisory psychologist for a Christian-based psychiatric hospital program called Rapha (which in Hebrew means "God heals"). I agreed to take the job before I was fully aware of how their treatment program operated. One of my jobs was to lead groups of staff members in discussion of the book, *The Search for Significance*, by Robert McGee[16], which is a biblically based approach to self-esteem. The staff then used this book as the basis for treatment of all Rapha's patients. Regardless of the admitting problem, the type of mental diagnosis, or life problem, all patients were required to work through this book. Of course, I was skeptical, but at least not so resistant this time. Sure enough, patients with all kinds of problems, including some I would have considered "chronic or untreatable," made tremendous progress.

What were the key factors to the remarkable success? Certainly prayer, faith, and reliance on the Holy Spirit would be valid responses. Yet, much of the success had to do with how people saw themselves in Christ. I should mention that the book also influenced my life and the lives of those on staff. Many people who struggle with individual problems (as well as marital problems) also struggle with their sense of self. More accurately, they feel that God is not pleased with them; as a result, they tell themselves many negative untruths. This negative self-talk in turn leads to ungodly and unhappy behaviors which create negative patterns. Negative thoughts and behavior patterns then form the basis for all kinds of life problems and mental disturbances. The solution is simple and biblical.

Christ Is the Answer

Christ is the solution to our self-esteem problems. Learning who we are in Christ is the key to our mental health. Realistically we are sinners. Yet, if we are believers, we are no longer under Christ's wrath and judgment. In short, God is pleased with us, accepts us, and loves us tremendously in Christ. Still, many Christians feel they must somehow earn God's approval. Intellectually, they may know they are "in Christ," yet in their thought lives and behavior they still try to live by self-imposed standards.

In Robert McGee's words, they tell themselves they must meet certain performance standards to be accepted by God, or they tell themselves that without the approval of certain people in their lives, they are not measuring up. If they cannot meet performance standards or win the approval of others, they blame everyone else for their plight, including God. Finally, they simply give up and label themselves as worthless and hopeless.

Some of the external worldly standards include having a great job, earning lots of money, getting all As in school, being the best athlete, being the most physically attractive, being able to buy expensive homes, cars, and clothes, being the head of all kinds of committees, or even being the pastor of a big church. Other people require the unconditional approval of others such as their spouse, family, church leaders, or friends.

Ask yourself, "For what or whom am I living?" You may find that your prime motivation is to meet certain performance standards or to win the approval of others, rather than realizing that God already loves you, accepts you as He made you, and even died for you.

In essence, we create false standards and gods, then live for them. We don't achieve these false standards, and then feel bad about ourselves in ways God never intended. Let me give you two quick examples.

One young lady who came to see me believed she was unacceptable unless she was thin. Her weight goals were unrealistic; therefore, she treated herself as a failure. She was obsessed with her perceived failing and was often depressed. She equated significance with thinness, when significance should come from Christ.

In another instance a pastor I treated equated success and significance with having a large church. He burnt himself out trying to win the approval of others and grow his congregation. This, too, was not the route to significance. God already loved and accepted him. The pastor made acceptance conditional to unrealistic goals he created for himself. He told himself he was a loser and often became angry and depressed.

I have noticed on many occasions in marriage counseling that usually one member of the couple is often either negative and angry, or sad and depressed. Usually the man is the angry one, and the wife is the depressed one. If what I am saying is correct, the fifth task of building your spouse's sense of significance will be crucial in terms of marriage transformation.

The Self Esteem of Your Spouse Matters

Ultimately, the needs we have for esteem and significance can only be met in Christ. This is a matter of faith. A Christian marriage starts with the premise that Christ is the center of married life. However, over the course of time, it is not uncommon for a spouse to struggle with self-esteem issues. The marriage relationship can be the means God uses to help spouses resolve self-esteem issues.

My wife had to help me in this area. My own initial reluctance to address self-esteem issues, described earlier in this chapter, was in a large part due to my own lack of comfort in my relationship with Christ. I had a strong tendency to get esteem and significance needs met by trying to obtain the approval of certain people in my life. My emotions tended to rise and fall based on perception of whether certain people (usually professors, church leaders, or successful men) approved of me. Thankfully, my wife was aware of this issue and gently helped redirect the source of my significance by doing a few things:

- She prayed for me.
- She supported me with statements such as, "Don, you don't need their approval."
- She challenged me with statements such as, "Don, you need to get over your need for their acceptance and look to Christ."

I see my wife's approach as a model to help other marriages. Wives can pray for their husbands, and then point out that husbands already have significance, through Christ. Wives can show their husbands they are loved, even if they don't make millions, aren't the pastor of a mega-church, or chief of police. If a husband is a believer, it is perfectly acceptable to emphasize that Christ loves and accepts him unconditionally, and regularly remind him of this fact. This may be one instance where a little nagging might actually be good, especially if the content is God's love. Lest you think this is unrealistic, I would point to the books I read in high school by Ann Kiemel. Ann was a young single, Spirit-filled woman living in Boston. Throughout her day, she would regularly greet strangers by saying, "God loves you and so do I." Many times, grown and apparently hardened men responded to her simple comments by breaking into tears. The public announcement of God's love is powerful in its ability to change lives. Such pronouncements should be heard regularly in a transformed Christian marriage. Make the task of proclaiming God's love of your spouse routine in your conversation.

Help Your Wife Find True Significance

Husbands need to pay particular attention to the issue of self-esteem in their wives. The Western media's standard of beauty is completely unrealistic in terms of its emphasis on youthfulness and thinness. The demand for youthful perfection is a crushing tyranny in the lives of many of our women. This oppression may exist in the mind of a woman who is viewed as relatively close to the standard of beauty or it may exist in the mind of a woman who is not near to that standard. The key issue is whether that woman is able to accept her body as God made her or if she feels shame because she is not "perfect."

Liberating your wife from the oppression of the perfection tyrant is certainly mission number one. A husband may not realize he has an important role to play in rescuing his wife from her own lies. Constant verbal assurance is important here. However, that assurance must not be fake. Most women can spot a faker a mile away.

Henry looked like a male model. He was about six feet, two inches tall and more "built" than that P90x guy on steroids. His face had classic features and he had great hair. Henry worked for the U.S. Secret Service, meaning he protected important political figures, but he wasn't supposed to talk about it. Cindy looked like she could easily double in a movie for the actress Cameron Diaz. She worked as a school teacher and I am certain every boy in her elementary school must have had a crush on her. They came to see me for marriage counseling, but their goals for seeking help were vague. There were no accusations of unfaithfulness, or complaints of any of the usual incompatibility issues. Henry said that Cindy didn't feel good about herself. Cindy agreed, and said she felt insecure about her appearance—she wasn't happy with her body. Henry believed this was nonsense, and continually tried to offer assurance that she was beautiful.

The problem with Henry's approach was twofold. First, he tended to be dismissive of Cindy's real feelings. What my wife says to me is never "nonsense." Due to our culture's emphasis on perfection, many attractive women suffer with problems of accepting of their bodies. The solution is to help our wives feel their significance in Christ just as He made them. But if we too quickly gloss over their own assessments (even if we don't agree with them), they won't believe our pronouncements.

If Cindy did not believe Henry heard her initially, then she doubted what he had to say to was real. She saw him as a fake. The second problem was that in this case, words alone were not all that mattered.

I met with Cindy alone and she said Henry did not take a leadership role at home. He seldom took initiative around the house and tended—despite his successful appearance—to be very passive. This was a turnoff to her. This is why it is so important for husbands to understand how the husband's role as prophet, priest, and king of the home relates to the improvement of his wife's self-esteem. Without biblical leadership in each of those roles, Henry's words were no different than what other men told her in the past. It's not like guys did not compliment her. But she needed her king to tell her he respected her. Since her king was not affirming her, she was tempted to get that affirmation from other males she respected. This situation puts a wife at risk for an affair.

As the priest of the home, the husband should pray for Christ to be the source of his wife's significance. He can also serve as a prophet by speaking God's truth regarding her heavenly Father's love for her. On a human level, he can simply demonstrate love. He can deliver in concrete form the love God offers spiritually. As a king, he can protect, defend, and support the queen of his home. This support is especially important if there are children at home, so he can model by his words and actions just how valuable she is to the home.

I once went to dinner with a lovely Christian family. I had an enjoyable time except for one observation. Most of the banter and jokes were mild mockeries of the mom. The children loved to tell jokes about the mom and she laughed along with them. The dad did not join in the banter, but was basically passive. I got the sense that this was a natural pattern that had gone on for years. Christian families ought to laugh and have fun, but the prophet, priest, and king should intervene to change the direction of the jokes into something more supportive of his wife's significance.

Douglas Wilson writes in his book, *Reforming Marriage*, that in a godly marriage, the wife, because she is valued by the loving husband and leader, will literally become more beautiful with time (a reflection of radiance of love bestowed, I suppose). The wife's self-esteem should improve in the context of a marriage transformed. Too many wives tell me their husbands are always putting them down. That should never be the case.

Assignment for Transformed Significance

Look up the following verses: Ephesians 1:7 and 2:5, 2 Corinthians 5:17, Jeremiah 31:3, and Romans 8:1, 17 and 37. Write down a summary of their content in your own words. For the summary of each verse, you can begin a sentence that starts with the sentence stem, "I am..." and then complete the sentence based on the content of the verse. As an example, for Ephesians 1:7, you could write, "I am forgiven."

What do these verses say about who we are in Christ? Discuss these findings with your spouse or write him or her a letter that lists what the Bible says about who he or she is in Christ. Use these verses as a basis of prayer and proclamation for your spouse.

Key Questions

1. Which partner in your marriage suffers more from low self-esteem? Discuss the ways you or your spouse feel insignificant. Is it from not meeting certain performance goals, not having the approval of another person who you value, or is it just a sense of helplessness?

2. What kind of thoughts do you speak to yourself, or does your spouse say, that reinforces the above feelings of insignificance? What could your spouse say or do that would specifically point you to the significance, love, and acceptance that is continually available in Christ? How could your spouse best remind you of God's love?

3. Husbands, are you fulfilling the roles of prophet, priest and king as they relate to your wife's self-esteem? If not, begin to apply yourself in all three areas. As another practical suggestion, try the following: Read Psalm 139 (in a modern paraphrase like the Living Bible) to your wife, speaking to

her in the second person. For instance, "You are fearfully and wonderfully made..."

THE SIXTH TASK:
Deal with Anger and Depression

> *My depression is the most faithful mistress I have known—no wonder, then, that I return the love.*
> —Soren Kierkegaard

In the introduction to this book I stated all marriages suffer under a curse since the fall of man. The contemporary outcome of the curse is that a man will try to dominate (often physically or monetarily) his wife and a wife will unconsciously or not-so-unconsciously try to control her husband. The gospel of Jesus Christ, when it is lived out by a husband fulfilling the tasks described in this book will help to reverse the curse in his marriage.

Reversing the curse in marriage is similar to John Milton's quote about repairing the ruins of our first parents—the repairs begin when we imitate Christ in our marriage. This of course is still subject to both the husband and wife being sinful and imperfect creatures. The fall of man negatively impacts our marriage in terms of relational dynamics. Moreover, it negatively impacts our lives in terms of our physical and emotional health. God wants us to redeem the relationship dynamics through the five tasks we've already covered as well as other means of becoming more like Christ.

In terms of emotional health, God wants to redeem two particular emotions, depression and anger. I also stated at the beginning of this book that men tend to get angry and women tend get depressed. Interestingly, these two emotions are simply the flip side of each other. Scratch the surface of an angry male and you find that deep down, or not so deep down, he is depressed about something important in his life. The depressed housewife probably is not able to express just what she is angry about. The complicating factor of marriage is that more often than not, those two emotions are directed toward our spouse. This may, or may not be shocking, but strong negative emotions toward our wife or husband are to be expected. Unfortunately, these emotions are often denied by some Christians, while for others, these emotions are seen as relationship failure.

Dealing with Anger

Book publishing is a precarious business these days. Small bookstores are a thing of the past. Books printed on paper seem to be going the way of the dinosaur. In such a climate, publishers tend to make safe choices about which books they will promote and invest resources. New authors have difficulty proving they will be successful prior to a work being published. New authors can attend writer's conferences to improve their writing, learn about the book market, and meet potential publishers. At writer's conferences authors can "pitch" their book ideas to an editor of a publishing house. I attended three such conferences and found them to be very helpful.

At one such event, I was pitching an early form of the book you are reading. I was told by the teachers at the conference to approach the publishers with a catchy title. So, I sat down with an editor of a Christian book publishing company. He was an older gentleman with a beard and fairly warm presence. He looked tired from his travels, worn out by listening to so many people and their dreams, all the while knowing that in today's market and economy not many would be realized.

I was more like Will Ferrell in the movie *Elf*. I was excited to talk to him about my half-written book. I told him I was a Christian psychologist, a married father of four, and I had written a marriage book to help my clients. He feigned genuine interest. He asked me what title I had in mind, which was my big chance to make a splash, so I said, *I Hate my Wife*.

I wish you could have seen his face. No doubt, he must have wondered what type of nutcase I was—the dangerous kind, the sick and demented kind, or the harmless and deluded kind. Then his face seemed to soften. He perceived that I wasn't crazy or malicious. He offered me some wise feedback.

"I don't think a Christian publisher would publish a book with that title, because it is likely to be misunderstood," he said. "However, I would want to publish a book which contained that title for one its chapters." The tired Christian publisher turned out to be a family man and was quite familiar the real emotional life of a marriage.

Anger and even depression get associated with sinful behavior so we tend to deny their existence. When Christians do talk about these emotions, they tend to give simplistic solutions, not dealing with the fact that these emotions can have deep roots. Secular writers often have a more realistic understanding of our darker natures (often too dark and hopeless). In the movie *Pretty Woman*, Richard Gere sits in a bathtub with Julia Roberts talking openly about his life. Gere's character says he is "angry" with his father, and it took three years of psychoanalysis just to be able to make that statement. Once we stop denying that we actually feel angry or depressed, we can begin to manage such emotions.

Quick, what is the answer to the following question: "Which is worse for your marriage, having sexual fantasies about your next door neighbor or fantasizing regularly about divorcing your spouse?" The answer is that both are equal on some weird scale and both are quite damaging. The question is also diagnostic. If you tend toward sexual fantasies about other women, then you have a lust problem. If you have divorce fantasies, then it is likely that you have an anger problem.

In the contemporary Christian community we are much more familiar discussing problem one, and in our sex saturated culture, the problems with lust are obvious. Moreover, the Bible repeatedly condemns sexual immorality. Perhaps, as a result, there is much less discussion of anger as a destroyer of marriage. I mentioned earlier that I attended a large Promise Keepers event. They set up a large tent in the middle of the stadium's football field and as men were convicted of a particular sin, they would enter the tent for individual confession and prayer. I was not in the tent, but I sensed from what I heard that the theme of most of the confessions had to do with sexual sins, especially pornography.

Recently, a famous evangelist/apologist was lecturing on the campus of a Bible college. He offered to meet with students after his talks for individual prayer. These "prayer meetings" ended up consuming each entire day as he listened over and over again to confessions of sexual sin. In public meetings, men burdened by guilt will confess problems with lust, pornography, fornication, and marital infidelity. The line to the tent labeled "anger" is considerably shorter, but it shouldn't be.

Issues with anger are much less obvious than lust. Lust is pretty obvious. A wife can point out that her husband never looks in her eyes at the restaurant because they are too busy following the waitresses' body parts around the serving aisles. She can check his history of sites visited on the internet and note how quickly he closes the screen when she walks in the room. The same applies for how quickly he flips the channel on the remote control when she walks in. He starts with denial, but that defense can be confronted by presenting internet search histories, credit card bills, and even phone bills. But anger is a much harder problem to confront. The only bill is an emotional one. The denial itself is angry rather shameful or contrite. This just makes it all the more unpleasant.

Victor had been a music minister of a large church for over a decade. His contemporary style, composition, and sound were amazing. His music program was a huge part of the church's success. After his band ripped, the pastor could give a "light" message and everyone went home happy, except for his band members. Great performances were met with even greater criticisms directed at the worship team members behind closed doors. On Tuesday night rehearsals you could actually hear Victor screaming if you were standing outside the church. Many talented musicians quit the band, but he could always find enough people with low enough self-confidence to follow their leader despite the abuse. That's until the pastor's wife joined the worship team.

At first, her complaints to her husband were registered by him as female hysteria. Guys are not good with emotions, even when they are pastors. Soon the pastor and his wife were having serious marital problems. It became clear the talented band leader had brought more than worship to the homes of his team. The pastor talked to the worship team leader about his anger, and not for the first time. He had heard the complaints many times before he heard them from his wife. The team leader denied his anger problem, expressed his anger toward the pastor, and they experienced their usual standstill.

Then, the pastor took an additional step. He spoke to the worship leader's wife. She started crying the minute he raised the issue. The worship team leader led his family in a tyranny of rage. They always walked on eggshells for fear of his outbursts. Their teenage daughter hated her dad. No one could talk to him. His denial was rooted in anger, but he just couldn't see his problem. The only reason his wife remained in the marriage was because her husband was a minister. The head pastor ordered the worship leader to visit with me.

Our meeting was brief. I told him about Moses. Moses represented salvation in the Old Testament and as such was a type of Jesus. Once he got angry and threw down his staff and God said he would not let him cross into the Promised Land. God is not an angry potentate and doesn't like it when His people misrepresent Him. A husband preaches Jesus to his family, and a worship leader preaches Jesus through his music, but when that man has an anger problem, he is lying about God. I told him the funny secret about the Bible and anger. God actually wants us to get angry. He wants us to be angry over our own sin. He wants us to be angry over the injustice in the world. He wants us to be angry when somebody takes advantage of widows and the poor. And he wants us to be angry when religious leaders live, act, and preach that God is a hothead, just like he was doing with his wife and kids. I told him his anger was sinful. The worship leader got up and left my office in silence. He returned the next week. I wasn't at all sure I would ever see him again. I had taken a risk and wondered if I had been too harsh. Instead, he told me he had a headache for two days after our meeting and ended up in bed as a result. He repented of his anger and he never went back to it again.

Most men are usually not aware they have these anger problems. In fact, most men are quite comfortable with their anger. The inside joke among counselor/therapist types is that anger is the only emotion that most men exhibit. All other emotions, including those related to sexuality stem from anger and its release. Anger is the one emotion that men believe is acceptable to express. When the anger is out of control, it tends to be evaluated subjectively. The worship team leader really believed his anger was an appropriate way to express leadership over his band and in his home. Question any angry man and you are likely to get this response (after he punches you in the nose), "So and so, or that situation, made me get angry," and "My response was called for and I would be a wimp if I didn't get angry." All anger is justified. Sadly, most anger looks a lot more like the frustration Moses showed than it does the righteous anger of Christ. Remember the last time you yelled and screamed at a family member? Now compare that to the last time you yelled and screamed that a widow in your church was treated poorly. The first example is sinful, and second rarely happens.

You may be breathing a sigh of relief at this point. You may say you do not have a rage problem, but there is another issue with anger that threatens your marriage. It is called negativity. If men have little insight into their anger, and if they justify their anger, and if they don't run down to the stadium tent to confess their anger, then it is even more likely that they give their general negativity a pass. Some marriages are dramatically torn apart by overt sexual sins and overt rage problems, but I suspect that even more marriages are slowly choked to death by negativity.

Here is a test. When you walk in the door at the end of work day is your wife happy to see you? If you don't get the big smile, it is easy to blame your wife. However, it might be more productive if you check your own attitude. Would you really be happy to see you? People generally respond well to positivity. Maybe you are not as positive as you think. Listen to how you talk to your wife.

Do you shoot down her ideas or make excuses about why you can't do what she is asking you to do? What kind of leadership or domestic support do you provide when you get home? She took care of the kids while you were at work and now she gets to take care of you as well. If you spend most evenings in front of the television, your computer, or your smart phone, then you have already failed this test. I call this the Zig Ziglar factor. Ziglar was a wildly successful salesman in the 1970s and '80s and then a noted motivational speaker for the next couple of decades. He said you should walk into your home with a big smile on your face and then you should look at your wife like she is the main attraction of the day. She is the destination. After you ask about her day and listen, really listen, the next thing out of your mouth ought to be, "Honey, how can I help you?" Find a way to answer your wife in the affirmative, even if you don't fully agree with her. Here are two comparative examples:

> Wife: I was thinking we should paint Suzy's room this weekend.
>
> Husband: You know I have plans this weekend to play golf and by the time we paint and let it dry it will take two days, and we have church duties on Sunday.
>
> Wife: I was thinking we should paint Suzy's room this weekend.
>
> Husband: That's a great idea. I already have golf plans in the morning. If you could get the paint supplies together, I could get started when I get back. We might not finish, but if you really want to do it we ought to try.

Another example:

> Wife: We really need to think about se nding Billy to the Christian school this year.
>
> Husband: That is not an option. You know we barely pay our bills as it is.
>
> Wife: We really need to think about sending Billy to the Christian school this year.
>
> Husband: We need to explore the possibility, but I am worried that we can't afford it. Do you have some ideas about how we can pay for it?

When the negative examples are repeated on a daily basis, over time a marriage is killed by inches. Most women are long-suffering, but on a human level their ability to put up with negative interactions is finite. When marriages end because of this, the wife often says she doesn't love her husband any more. The husband is simply bewildered because he has no insight into his negativity.

Terry was one of my most memorable clients. He was an airline industry executive who was materially successful with a large home on the water and a boat out back that would quickly take him to the Atlantic Ocean. On an emotional level he was a wreck. Often flying into irrational rages at home and even became physical toward his wife. She called the police at least twice. As a bright man, he was intellectually aware of his problem. His wife moved out after the latest incident, fearing for her own safety. So Terry enrolled in the County's anger management program. It was populated by other court-ordered males. He was the only man in the group who was not court ordered.

Terry completed the program, but still had anger problems at home, so he enrolled in the program again. The facilitator made him co-leader and he was often in the position of having to protect the leader (a female, if you can believe it) from the angry male clients. He did not really improve. So he came to see me. I met with him and his wife. Terry was an intimidating presence, naturally giving off a vibe that he needed to be handled with care. His fuse was quite short. It turned out that he learned all of his anger growing up at home. I won't go into details because it was not a pretty picture. Anger and intimidation had worked well for him in sports, the military, and even in corporate business. It did not work well at home. He had a lot of guilt over the pain he caused his wife and family. Terry tried to live as a Christian, but kept failing.

The director of the counseling center where I work says, "Hurt people, hurt people." This was the case with Terry. We developed a good working relationship, but finally I had to tell him he needed to go for a more intensive program. He eventually found the local Life Skills International program, which is a Christian-based domestic violence program created by a former domestic abuser named Paul Hegstrom. Terry was able to transform his life over the course of many months. He even became a board member of the local organization. Sometimes anger runs deep. For some, it is literally lodged deep in the structures of the brain.

Neuroscience research indicates that some men with violent anger problems have a problem in their amygdala, a very small structure at the top of spinal column. It is positioned underneath the gray matter, which we generally think of as our brain. The gray matter, is what gives us a personality, the ability to think, to process things, and to make sound judgments. The frontal lobe at the top and front of our brain is what allows us to be civilized humans and not animals. The lower part of the brain at the top of the spinal column (known as the brainstem) has a completely different function than the gray matter. The brainstem bypasses all the thinking, judging, and processing of the gray matter above and focuses on the basic functioning of the body—heart rate, breathing, waking up, and being conscious.

If humans only had brainstems, they would function at a very instinctual level, like animals. We are not aware of our brainstems in action, but if the brainstem was not running in the background, we would be in a coma or dead. The amygdala warns the body of external danger. It is responsible for the body's "fight or flight" response. If you run into a bear in the woods, the amygdala will immediately send adrenaline rushing into your body so you can flee. If a man is approached by an attacker, the amygdala will tell him to fight. So, our survival depends on the amygdala's ability to respond in less than a second. If the gray matter were to get involved, there would be too much delay. The amygdala says, "Go!" while the gray matter says, "Let's think about this."

War trauma and early childhood traumas may kindle an overactive amygdala. The gray matter gets bypassed and every little incident in life is read as a red alert. Since the gray matter is bypassed, all the talking in the world won't change this problem. I could never have told Terry to "knock it off," like I did to the worship leader. He went to group therapy twice! Terry had a physiological problem, but surgery and medication is not the ideal treatment. Retraining the amygdala to respond differently is the answer. Eventually, it learns to calm down and only fire when there is a real threat, not because someone moved your car keys. This kind of anger problem requires specialized forms of therapy that focus on retraining the brain.

Terry wanted to save his marriage, so he kept working on the problem until he found a solution. In essence, Terry used the energy from his anger to keep pursuing a solution that finally curtailed his anger problem. If you have an anger problem, do not let pride stop you from getting the help you need.

Dealing with Depression

George had a dream job. He was a radar repairman for large cruise ships. At the time, there were only a handful of people who could do his job. As a result, he was in high demand and could set his own hours. All he had to do was show up for work and he was paid handsomely. If the ship was on a Caribbean island or at sea, they would pay to fly him to the ship. Things were great until one day when George could not get out bed. He wasn't sick. He was depressed. George could not tell you why which just made the situation all the more frustrating.

Over time his customers stopped calling him because he wasn't showing up for work. Bills mounted. His wife became exasperated and they fought. George's sister was able to talk George into seeking Christian counseling. The counselor at the church recommended prayer and had some positive suggestions, but George was still missing work—something he had almost never had done in the past. I saw George after that and believed his problem to be more physiological than something psychological.

George went to a family physician and then to a psychiatrist who prescribed antidepressant medication. This helped George get back to work, but he became too hyper. His wife and kids noticed a temper in him that was not consistent with who he was before he began taking the medication. It took a while for the medication to be sorted out and it was not an easy or instant process. Eventually, he began a course of therapy that included something called cognitive-behavioral therapy. This therapy began to systematically change George's thinking patterns. In time, with a combination of medication and targeted psychotherapy, he was able to get back to work.

Although the process was not easy, there was the additional benefit of spiritual growth. George said his mental anguish led him to seek the Lord. Additionally, changing his thinking resulted in renewing his mind in a way that allowed him to better understand his relationship to a God who loved him with an everlasting love.

If you have ever suffered from depression, then you have also struggled with being misunderstood. Depression, because it is emotional, is often regulated to the realm of the mysterious, the superstitious, and the vaguely sinful. Here are some responses from the bad advice column. There are some Christians who will tell you to "just get over it." They believe in American individualism and they believe that Christianity equals hard work—it's a "pull yourself up by your own bootstraps" type of religion. While hard work is commended in the Bible, at times we have to completely rely on the Lord to save us. Medical problems and depression are things that ultimately only God can heal. All of our hard work comes to naught if God doesn't choose to heal. Just putting our hands to the plow will not always resolve our feelings of depression.

Essentially, aside from not being caring or empathetic, people who espouse the "just get over it" approach are in reality, Deists. Deism is a worldview in which people believe in God as the creator and head of the universe, but not intimately and personally involved in the lives of humans. They see God as handling the big issues, but not your personal depression. Biblical Christianity on the other hand makes it clear that God, in the form of Jesus, cares intimately about every little matter in our lives. God knows about your depression and He has a direct purpose for its existence in your life.

While the first group of bad advisors is decidedly uncaring, the next group is worse. These Christians will tell you to "repent from it." Such spiritual Pharisees know for certain that a specific sin in your life is the cause of the depression. John 9:1-7 contains a story about a man who was born blind that speaks to this very issue:

> Now as Jesus passed by, He saw a man who was blind from birth. And His disciples asked Him, saying, "Rabbi, who sinned, this man or his parents, that he was born blind?"
>
> Jesus answered, "Neither this man nor his parents sinned, but that the works of God should be revealed in him. I must work the works of Him who sent Me while it is day; the night is coming when no one can work. As long as I am in the world, I am the light of the world."
>
> When He had said these things, He spat on the ground and made clay with the saliva; and He anointed

the eyes of the blind man with the clay. And He said to him, "Go, wash in the pool of Siloam" (which is translated, Sent). So he went and washed, and came back seeing.

The message is pretty straightforward, the Pharisees assume that specific sin is behind the man's blindness. Jesus says the blindness has nothing to do with sin, but some events happen for God's purposes. It's more about God than the specifics of sin. After the healing, the real misunderstanding begins. What follows could be read as comedy if it weren't so tragic. The Pharisees threaten the healed man's parents and then they excommunicate the previously blind man from the church, all because he will not deny the obvious, that Jesus healed him. The Pharisees were focused on the details of the law and sin and therefore could not see the greater purposes of God, such as healing and salvation.

Depression versus the Weight of Sin

Some sins do bring with them their own special sense of guilt and shame. Most people who are caught up with these sins do not need this connection to be pointed out. They get it. What these sufferers need to understand is that by repenting and forsaking those behaviors they receive automatic and complete forgiveness. Some people struggle with forgiving themselves. Of course, it is God who heals and it is God who forgives, so these people need to be encouraged to stop trying to forgive themselves and see themselves as God sees them; as His beloved and precious children. Often, just by changing what we say to ourselves, we can make great strides with our depression. Review these scripts and see which one would work better at causing depression:

God hates me. God is angry at with me for sinning. God can never forgive me for my sins. I just can't be forgiven. I can never do enough. I will never be pleasing to God.

God loves me. God poured out all His wrath and anger on Jesus on the cross, so He is happy with me because of Jesus. God tossed all my sins in the sea of forgetfulness. Nothing can separate me from the love of Christ. I am child of God, a member of His kingdom,

and fully pleasing to Him. There is nothing I can do to
make God love me more or love me less. Jesus loves me.

We work ourselves into significant depression by playing the
first set of scripts in our head. But we can we can make great
progress with feelings of depression if we play the second set of
scripts instead. The Bible has positive things to say about those
who put their faith in Jesus Christ. Colossians 1:9-16 and Romans
8:28-37 are two encouraging passages that fit well with the second
script. I often have my clients take the above phrases or verses of
the Bible and write them on 3x5 cards and post them around the
house and in their car so they will begin the habit of the saying
these helpful scripts to themselves.

If you still think sin is at the heart of your depression then you
need to study the gospel. Jesus' redemption forgives us and even
redeems us from the curse.

Some Christians who suffer from depression face a double
whammy. They suffer the real pain of depression then they suffer
from the spiritual misdiagnoses of the problem. It has always been
amazing to me that modern day Pharisees rarely diagnose physical
health problems as sin, while nearly always diagnosing mental
health problems as such.

Bad advisors regarding depression don't just come in the form
of those who say "get over it" and modern day Pharisees who say
"repent from it." The third group of bad advisors are people who
believe medication is the sufficient solution to depression. This
group operates from an experiential basis. Either they or someone
they know has successfully treated depression through the use of
antidepressant medication. Antidepressant medication is no better
or worse than other types of medications for physical conditions,
but all medications must be used advisedly.

When a person takes medication for depression, he or she
must consider two issues.

First, they may neglect to address the underlying causes of the
problem. When adults get diabetes, they can take medications to
get their blood sugars under control, but some also need to address
the underlying causes of their condition. In this case, it may be that
the adult onset diabetes is caused by lifestyle factors like a poor
diet and lack of exercise. Medication is helpful and even needful,

but it should not supplant the exploration of causes that could eliminate the problem in the first place.

The second issue is that there is the lemming-like approach to the use of antidepressant medications. It seems like everyone uses them and it seems like almost any type of medical doctor prescribes them. According to the Center for Disease Control and Prevention about 11% of the U.S. population over age 12 is taking anti-depressant medications[18], so it might be important to consider whether or not these are simply being prescribed by default. Antidepressant medications affect mood and sexual function, sometimes adversely, so there is a need for caution in the use of these medications. Part the problem is the popularity and success of these medications. Often antidepressants are prescribed by doctors who do not specialize in their use.

If someone has a physical heart condition, he or she needs to be under the care of a cardiologist. Cardiologists know from experience which drugs are best for which conditions. They understand and anticipate side effects and they know when to adjust dosage amounts or when to change the type of medication all together. It is a complicated matter that takes years of training. It is no different with antidepressant medications. In 2005, only 29% of these prescriptions were written by psychiatrists who are specialists trained in these medications. The rest of these medications were written by general practitioners (23%), family practitioners (21%), internal medicine specialists (10%), and other sources[19]. This can lead to people having unnecessarily bad experiences with these medications.

Antidepressants are not addictive, despite what has been reported at times, but these medications need to be closely monitored by competent psychiatrists. Negative side effects, interactive effects with other drugs, and rebound side effects when people come off them are all realities.

Medications are popular because they are often effective. But sometimes counseling can be a better solution to the problem of depression. Counseling can be done with and without the use medications. One specific type of counseling that I mentioned earlier, called cognitive behavioral therapy (CBT) has been shown in research studies to be very effective in treating depression. CBT has about the same effectiveness as medications. A combination of medication and CBT has the highest rate of effectiveness. However, CBT alone is effective, and it has the advantage of avoiding side effects. CBT and other types of effective counseling gives those who suffer the skills to deal directly with depression and thereby treat the problem at its source. The counseling approach to depression is so advantageous that one author has said the prescribing of medication without a recommendation for counseling is now unethical[20]. My point is that it is bad advice to simply throw a pill at the problem, however medication with therapy when properly monitored can be very effective.

The fourth group of bad advisors, people who only trust natural remedies, often make it their business to make sure you don't use traditional medications to treat depression. On the positive side, they tend to be health conscious. For these naturalist advisors, the Bible becomes a health manual and that eliminates newer types of medical interventions but still accepts natural remedies as instructed by certain Bible passages. The efforts of this group are admirable, especially when they are consistent in their beliefs. For instance, if they favor natural remedies in all circumstances because of their beliefs and trust the Lord for healing, that is commendable. However, this can go off the rails in two ways—such as when only certain illnesses are singled out for natural remedies or when their unique theological conviction is elevated to an inflexible creed. In this second case, these advisors become apostles of the natural. Those who suffer from depression and who do not agree with this approach to health are made to feel like sinners. Hence, this approach can encourage all manner of healthy lifestyle choices which in turn can be of great benefit to those who suffer from depression, but it can also morph into people feeling condemned for their depression by a new type of health Pharisee.

Enough about the bad advice. Here is some good advice. If you want to save your marriage, take your problem with depression seriously. As my wife would say, "Stop being a slump." Notice that all of the six tasks discussed in this book require action—even the task of avoiding. Suffering from depression, which can go on for many years, limits your ability to fulfill the tasks.

Wives find that living with a depressed, and hence, negative, passive, inert, or "slumpy" husband to be particularly difficult. Few people realize that many marriages end in divorce due to depression. We are well aware of dramatic endings, in which a spouse leaves after affairs, addictions, or abuse. Those endings stand out in our minds. Marriages that end because of depression are quiet, sad events, much like the illness that is the cause.

Of course, many Christian wives are willing to be long-suffering and live a life of quiet desperation. They know that God hates divorce, but real frustration occurs when a husband does not take responsibility to treat his depression. If the husband had cancer, both the husband and the wife would receive all kinds of support, including prayers, elder visits, and home cooked meals. When depression strikes home none of the above can be expected. I have seen this played out many times in Christian homes. Often these couples will not seek marital counseling because the husband's illness leaves him passive and unhopeful. He does not see the connection between his depression and his marriage.

Susan and Bill were separated. They had been separated previously, and then reunited for several years after seeking counsel from their pastor. As their counselor, I attempted to reproduce what had worked for them in the past. Unfortunately, Susan was resistant to returning to live with Bill because he refused to address his own depression. She had dreams and ideas about what a marriage should be like. Her expectations centered on her husband being proactive in their relationship. She dreamed of intimacy, talks, dates, and activities as a family. Bill could only manage to focus on his work and even that was overwhelming and consuming for him. He had nothing else to give. He was depressed, hopeless, critical, and inflexible. He was particularly hurt because his wife had abandoned him.

We met over many months but the issues were always the same—Bill did not want to make any changes, but he did want Susan to return. Susan had returned home once before but left again after Bill would not make any changes. After a while they stopped seeing me. I don't know how things turned out for them. Yet, I have no doubt they would have reunited if Bill had taken responsibility for his depression.

If and when their marriage finally ends in a legal sense, Susan will most likely take the blame for not being Christian enough to stick with her covenant vow of marriage. Bill may blame himself for being too caught up in his work, although he will quickly point out that he had no choice in the matter. In neither case will Bill's depression be seen as the cause—a cause that is treatable. I am aware that both Bill and Susan harbor sinful attitudes. Susan's leaving the marriage may be the most obvious, but Bill had the power in his hands to save his marriage.   Depression   in   a husband is something that must be dealt with directly. The six tasks of a contemporary marriage are embedded in an anti-passive lifestyle; depression creates passivity. Depression often masks itself in anger, produces negativity and hopelessness, and saps the husband of all his strength. Emotions are very narrow or there is no emotion. The couple will have little energy for a sex life or the romance related to sexuality. And usually sleeping and eating problems are part of the equation as well. Despite the stereotype, people with serious depression usually do not sleep all the time. Instead, they suffer from insomnia. They don't sleep at night and therefore they are exhausted and lethargic during the day. Their thoughts are often dark and negative. Those thoughts must be explored because if a person with depression becomes suicidal, immediate attention and assessment must be made. Sometimes hospitalization is required.

Drake had not slept well for months. He was often on edge and his family walked on eggshells. He worked, came home, and had dinner with his family. He rarely interacted with his wife, Sylvia, or their kids. After dinner, he retreated to his room alone to watch TV until he fell asleep early. He would wake up a couple of hours later and was unable to get back to sleep. He tossed and turned. He would get up, eat more, watch TV and surf the internet again. He did not view pornography and had no interest in sex.

Sylvia urged him to see his family doctor. His doctor prescribed medications for sleeping and depression but he quit taking them before they could work properly or before the right dosage or medication could be adjusted. He dismissed all medication interventions. He also refused counseling because in his mind, his main problems are work pressures and insomnia.

One day, Sylvia had good news. Their son had been chosen for a select traveling soccer team. She planned to share it with Drake over dinner in the hopes of cheering him up since she knew he used to be an avid sports fan.

"Drake, I have great news! Coach Evan called and said that Marcus has been selected for the elite travel club. Isn't that super?"

"Great. How are we going to pay for that? The travel team is much more expensive. Plus we have to spend more time with the Henderson's and Hardin's."

Sylvia tried not to give into his negativity. "I hadn't thought of that dear, but I just thought you would want to be excited for Marcus. It's a great accomplishment. They even picked Marcus over Reid Wilson to be on the team."

Drake, raised his voice. "I know you may not have thought about the cost and the time and also the extra commitment and extra running around, but I did. I am always the one who has to think of everything in this house. Why can't you see how difficult this will make things? I need to go lie down and get some rest. You can figure out how we can pay for all this good news."

There could be a whole host of reasons as to why Drake is so negative. Many counselors would say this is just his personality style, but I would say treating his depression may very well change his outlook. Here are some things to consider:

1. Everybody gets depressed at some point. Depression is a common problem and in most cases it is a passing experience. Even cowboys get the "blues." People can actually snap out of it, but if it persists, then it must be addressed. Work stress is often a big part of the problem. If that is the case, then change must be focused in that direction. If insomnia is the problem, then that should be dealt with directly. Sometimes there is a personal sin issue, or a doubt related to faith—this should be addressed by a pastor or a spiritually mature counselor. When a depressed mood interferes with a person's normal level of functioning at home or at work, it is time to consider intervention.

2. Not all depressions are the same and that is what makes it so confusing.

a. Bipolar depression is characterized by periods of mania (excessive activity, high energy, euphoria, or an unrealistic mood) so at times these sufferers are the opposite of depressed. After the mania, they shift into deep depression. The mania usually lasts a short time and the depressed period often lasts for months. This is a serious form of mental illness. There is much evidence that this disorder has genetic roots, meaning it runs in families. Of all the types of depression, this one especially requires good psychiatric care. In particular, these sufferers are most at risk to be suicidal. On the flip side, this type of depression can often be successfully treated with medication.

b. Major depression is characterized by negative moods and a lack of pleasure from experiences that used to be pleasurable. Sufferers of major depression have little or no energy. They will not initiate activities at home. Their sex life will disappear. If they used to enjoy playing golf or eating out at restaurants, they will have no interest whatsoever in these things, and they will decline participation even when others initiate the activities. They may retreat from life and spend long periods of time in bed. Again, both counseling and medication should be considered. Generally, sufferers will be reluctant to seek help because they often have a hopeless and negative outlook. When they do seek help, the changes can be quite dramatic. They are likely to get over their depression with a proper diagnosis and help.

c. Mild depression and chronic low level depression are often harder to diagnose and treat. Counseling can help and medication should not be the first avenue of intervention. Pastoral help, marriage counseling, and the accountability of the Christian community can make a big difference. If the depression is mild, encouragement can help.

d. Postpartum depression hits a new mother suddenly. Some medical conditions in men can also produce sudden depression. In both cases a good medical examination is recommended. In the case of George above, I made sure he had seen his doctor before therapy started.

e. Finally, when people face losses they experience a type of depression known as grief. Here the best approach is a combination of understanding and support. They need the presence of others, but not the advice or judgment of others. See the book of Job in the Bible for examples of how not to help sufferers of loss. When people face loss, they go through periods of anger as well. Often there is a fluctuation between both emotions. Grief can last for months, but it should not last forever. Support groups have been known to help grief sufferers.

3. From all of the above, it should be clear that one solution does not fit all. It's complicated. Moreover, the fact that it is complicated means that any solution will require a concerted effort. Spouses and loved ones of a sufferer often end up working hard to get their loved one much needed help. There may be periods of failure as well as success, so it is important not to get discouraged.

4. If you are the one suffering from depression, it is important to realize that getting your spouse to change will not make you feel better. Since we tend to sinfully blame our spouses for all sorts of things, it is often the case that husbands blame them for their own depression. Depression is the problem, not your wife. Fix your depression and then get marital counseling, in that order.

5. Lastly, keep in mind that all depression goes in cycles, like much of God's created world. Depression is often our body's way of forcing us to slow down and learn about ourselves. It can force us to look squarely at issues in our marriage. It can force us to consider whether we are leading healthy lifestyles with the right combinations of rest, exercise, and diet. If there is something out of balance in our lives, depression can shine a spotlight on that problem. God is sovereign and often sends depression and illness, much like the man who was born blind for His greater purposes. Those purposes can include our learning to trust our Savior all the more despite periods of depression. In the past, the saints of the church used to recite long passages from the Bible and lines from hymns to sustain them in periods of depression. The words of the following Swedish hymn, *Day by Day and with Each Passing Moment*, by Carolina V. Sandell-Berg (1865) has been especially helpful to me when I have been depressed. The tune can be found online, the lyrics are reproduced below[21]:

> Day by day, and with each passing moment,
> Strength I find to meet my trials here;
> Trusting in my Father's wise bestowment,
> I've no cause for worry or for fear.
> He, whose heart is kind beyond all measure,
> Gives unto each day what He deems best,
> Lovingly its part of pain and pleasure,
> Mingling toil with peace and rest.
> Every day the Lord Himself is near me,
> With a special mercy for each hour;
> All my cares He fain would bear and cheer me,
> He whose name is Counsellor and Pow'r.
> The protection of His child and treasure
> Is a charge that on Himself He laid;
> "As thy days, thy strength shall be in measure,"
> This the pledge to me He made.
> Help me then, in every tribulation,
> So to trust Thy promises, O Lord,
> That I lose not faith's sweet consolation,
> Offered me within Thy holy Word.

> Help me, Lord, when toil and trouble meeting,
> E'er to take, as from a father's hand,
> One by one, the days, the moments fleeting,
> Till with Christ the Lord I stand.

If you are experiencing anger or depression, talk to your pastor, then maybe a medical doctor to see if there is an underlying condition that is making you angry or depressed. Next seek mental health counseling. Make sure that the counselor is a Christian, but also make sure he or she has professional credentials. Investigate the counselor's level of experience with your problem area. Ask for references. If medications are suggested, make sure that their use will be monitored by a psychiatrist who is competent.

If your wife is the one who suffers from anger or depression, her greatest need is your support, not your correction, blame, or even advice. First, practice the tasks outlined in this book. Second, look closely at the fifth task in this book and make sure you are helping to build her significance. Most likely she carries an extra burden of guilt for experiencing anger or depression. She must be reminded of her forgiveness through the work of Christ. Third, if the problem continues, follow the steps above related to pastoral, medical, and professional help.

Key Questions

Dealing with emotions is a difficult topic for most men. It is unchartered waters. Also it is difficult to know ourselves and how we come across to others and even our spouses. Therefore these critical questions should be asked of your spouse when you are in a frame of mind to receive some honest answers. If you are in a difficult marriage and you do not believe your wife can give you feedback without a fight erupting, then ask a trusted friend these questions. If you develop insight into the fact that you indeed have a problem with anger or depression this revelation should be shared with your wife.

1. Do I come across as someone who angers easily? Be honest.

2. Why aren't you happy when I come through the door at the end of the day? What could I change that would make you happy to see me?

3. Are you ever frightened by my behavior or actions? What specifically do I do that is scary?

4. Would you say I am more the explosive angry type or the chronically negative type? Share some examples of what I do that is either angry or negative.

5. Do I have a problem in any of these areas: sleep (too much or too little), eating (too much or too little), lack of enjoyment in things that I should enjoy or used to enjoy, lack of interest in normal sexual relationships, chronic lack of energy, or negative thinking? If so, do you believe I suffer from depression?

6. Do you think it would make a big difference in our marriage if I pursued help for anger or depression?

Create A New Model
of Family Life

Why do farmers farm, given their economic adversities on top of the many frustrations and difficulties normal to farming? And always the answer is: "Love. They must do it for love." Farmers farm for the love of farming. They love to watch and nurture the growth of plants. They love to live in the presence of animals. They love to work outdoors. They love the weather, maybe even when it is making them miserable. They love to live where they work and to work where they live. If the scale of their farming is small enough, they like to work in the company of their children and with the help of their children. They love the measure of independence that farm life can still provide. I have an idea that a lot of farmers have gone to a lot of trouble merely to be self-employed to live at least a part of their lives without a boss.

—Wendell Berry, *Bringing it to the Table: Writings on Farming and Food*

He was lying in bed. A large man, he must have been at least ninety years old. Age had removed his ability to see. Despite his age and infirmities, I had a certain dread when I approached his virtually empty room. I knew little of the man personally, yet he still radiated an aura of gravitas or importance even as he rested quietly in the nursing home where I was working as an orderly for the summer. That man, who I will call Reverend Baker, was dying well. Walking into his room, one sensed peace and contentment—qualities that were contrary to my youthful college years at the time. The juxtaposition between his peaceful character and my own unsettled heart made me quite nervous as I passed the threshold into his room. His voice was deep, aged, and somewhat hollow.

"My tape has stopped, my tape has stopped," he said to no one in particular. He repeated himself. He wasn't impatient, he was just informing those who might be working in the area. I walked in the room and took care of the request. My hands nervously fumbled with the cassettes to be replaced. He spent his time listening to sermons, Bible readings, and hymns. He thanked me. He then returned to a state of meditation. What was the source of his peace? I wrestled with this question and it resulted in some surprising observations about family.

Many of the people in the nursing home had few to no visitors. The loneliness was suffocating. It was so pervasive it permeated the walls. The smell that confronted you when you walked in the front doors of the nursing facility wasn't that of basic human functioning, it was the smell of isolated humanity. The staff worked diligently to meet the basic physical needs of the residents, however there was only one thing that could mitigate the experience of isolation in a nursing home—family. I made a vow, then and there, that I would create a life in which, should I ever be a nursing home resident, my family would want to visit me.

While many residents lacked visitors, others had visitors, but those visitors usually fell into one of two categories— uncomfortable or anxious. Uncomfortable visitors visited out of obligation. They weren't sure what to do and they were in a hurry to leave. They tended to interact more with the staff or look at the ubiquitous TV in the room. They avoided direct eye contact with the resident. They often looked at their watch. You could tell they did not have a good relationship with the resident. Perhaps, they were fulfilling a family obligation or church obligation to visit, but they were not close with the person. Most likely they never were that close.

The anxious visitors showed a lot of concern over the residents, spending more time with them. They complained to the staff. They fussed over the resident, but still there was no closeness. Often the resident would talk about him or herself but the anxious visitors weren't listening. They had their own agendas. They wanted to take the resident out to the patio, but it was a big production and required input and attention from staff. It wasn't natural or organic, because it was more about the selfish issues of the visitor than actual needs of the resident.

Reverend Baker had an elderly daughter and mature attractive granddaughters who attended his bedside. His daughter came regularly and sat quietly with him, but his granddaughters were the ones who made an impression on my young mind. They brought their families and they seemed happy to be there. They all crowded into the room and talked amongst themselves. You could tell they were used to being in their grandfather's presence and being comfortable in his presence. This was balanced by a certain air of respect. Based on their attire, it was clear that all lived lives of more than adequate provision. There were no anxious concerns, they were people of faith. Not uncomfortable, indeed they acted just like I imagine they did at home. The aroma emanating from that room was contentment and love, never the stench of loneliness.

Working backward from the end of Revered Baker's life caused me to speculate what kind of family life would lead to peace and contentment rather than loneliness and anxiety. Some of the elements were obvious; faith, love, and a certain amount of provision. The focus of this chapter is on how to create an atmosphere where those elements can flourish.

A Transformed Model

To get to the end of life and truly be successful, we need a guiding model of family life—a standard by which to make comparisons. Models are hard to come by in our postmodern age. If someone has a model of what a family should look like, it tends to be very individualistic. Perhaps it is made up as the family develops through life, or perhaps the guiding principle is very simple, "Let's not raise our kids the way our parents raised us!" If there is no model of a good functional family, then there is a good chance the biblical principles related to family life will be missed.

Growing up in the church and attending youth groups in the 1970s and '80s, a model was clearly presented to me by people in those settings as the biblical model. That model is the one commonly known as the "breadwinner-homemaker" model. In this model, the husband, alone, is the main financial provider while the wife stays at home and raises the children. This model was popular in American society in the 1950s. Somehow the biblical idea of family structure melded into the American dream of family structure. The only problem with this model is that it does not look like the families presented in the Bible. It is also a sure-fire way to end up lonely in the nursing home.

Sole Provision

There is nothing wrong with providing financially for your family. Previously, I quoted the apostle Paul who said, "If anyone does not provide for his own, and especially his household, he has denied the faith and is worse than an unbeliever," (1 Timothy 5:8). I noted that Reverend Baker appeared to have provided well for his family. The Bible speaks often of provisional blessing. Many of the people recorded in the Bible were wealthy; such Abraham, Solomon, Job, and in the New Testament, Joseph of Arimathea, and Lydia, the Philippian businesswoman.

On the other hand, the Bible has many clear warnings not to make provision our primary goal in life. Many godly people in the Bible would be considered impoverished by American standards, including Jesus. Money can easily become an idol. Jesus made that point well when he said, "It is easier for a camel to go through the eye of a needle then for a rich man to enter the kingdom of heaven (Mark 10:25, Matthew 19:24)."

Herein lies the problem. To be the sole financial provider of a family in the present economy, a man would need to work exceedingly hard. So hard, that the goal itself often becomes obsessive by default. So much energy is invested in acquiring financial wealth that marriage and family needs are neglected. Perhaps, someone would argue that they would not let the quest for money crowd out their commitment to family, but that has not been the case in many of the families I have counseled. It is not the lack of money that has been the problem, but the husband's pursuit of money to the detriment of marriage and family involvement.

What do children learn when they observe their father's financial quest for significant amounts of money? They learn to value money and material possessions over relationship. When the successful husband becomes elderly, his children can afford to send to him the nursing home and have no guilt about not visiting.

In a sense, materialism creates the isolated prison (albeit a comfortable prison) of his last years.

Of course, not all sole providers are successful. Many of my clients have spent their middle years plowing their working lives into businesses that did not turn a profit, or that crashed in one way or another. These men reap the bitter harvest of financial failure and relationship failure. The successful sole financial provider or business owner looks like the possessor of the American Dream in the breadwinner-homemaker model. He will probably be made an elder in the church, but unless he is a rare individual, under the surface lurks a household that is not "well-managed."

Compartmentalization

By definition, the sole provider will go off to work while his wife is at home. This begins the potential problem of a division of labor that can be unbiblical. The Bible calls husbands to be involved in the instruction of both their wives and children. This requires a close relationship. The sole provider who is successful can afford private schooling to educate his children. School, sports, and extracurricular activities create different worlds for the father and his children. Interaction time is reduced to minutes a day. Modern church does not help since children have their own programs. Wealthier wives can hire others (like maids or even nannies) to help create their own leisure space and therefore develop their own lives and interests apart from their husband and children. In less well-off families, the wife is expected to maintain all domestic work and childcare. This leads directly to bitterness, especially when the husband is not able or is unwilling to share that burden.

It may be that the reason so many marriages end in divorce today is not just due to a lack of communication, sex, or finances, but an unsustainable model of family life. In Genesis, we read that Eve was created to be a helpmate for Adam. She was taken from his rib, she was "bone of my bone, flesh of my flesh." She was created to work side-by-side with Adam. There is no compartmentalization here. Together they worked in the garden. No other created being was a suitable partner.

The industrial age in the late 1700s into the mid-1800s moved the family into separate spheres with husbands and wives working outside the home for wages. Work outside of the home became the focus of life. Not family life. This has been the on-going tension for the last 150 years. Whether the husband, wife, or both work outside the home, it begs the questions—how much of a focus and priority is marriage and family life?

An Agrarian Model of Family Life

I would propose an older model for the new problems facing contemporary marital life. I would call that model the agrarian (which means "relating to rural matters") model and suggest that it is the closest to the biblical model of family life. In the Old Testament, most families were agrarian or farm-based. When we get to the New Testament, we also see merchants, craftsmen (carpenters), producers (vineyard owners, fishermen), and even wage earners (day laborers along with slaves). These additional classes were still close to the land and nature as well as the symbolic meanings and metaphors consistent with agrarian society. Also, if the husband worked a craft, his wife was usually close at hand with the children involved in what constituted a family enterprise.

I further suggest that the values produced by farm families, with their individually owned farms were a precursor of Thomas Jefferson's conceptualization of American democracy. Individually owned farms produced unprecedented individuality but farmers had to meet and work together for the common good. This was the beginning of the public square and it produced a unique set of values. Thomas Jefferson feared imported goods from Europe because the desire for material goods might undermine the pure ideal of independent and interdependent farming.

The values related to the farming community has been extolled by writer/poet/farmer Wendell Berry. Berry speaks of the values produced by farming in spiritual terms. The esteemed Harvard political philosopher Michael J. Sandel has said that the idea of the common good stems from a set of values consistent with the American farming ideal and in reality are very close to classical Christian values[22].

Despite being very "old school," this agrarian model has a current appeal. The farming "ideal" has a strong pull. Notice that Zynga, the company that makes the Facebook game, Farmville, is worth billions of dollars. Notice too, that Ree Drummond's blog, "The Pioneer Woman" is one of the more popular blogs on the web[23]. That site describes her life as someone who had been raised in a suburban environment, but who now enjoys being a rural farm wife, a homeschooling mom, and the author of traditional cookbooks. This ideal has great appeal and she comes across as very industrious and fulfilled in her life. I would suggest that the concepts of the agrarian life can be translated to the average American family without having to move to the farm as did Ms. Drummond.

The agrarian model produces a set of values that seem aptly biblical. Those values are dependence on God, teamwork, children are valued, democratic leadership in the home, much less focus on entertainment, and non-rigid gender roles.

Dependence on God

To run a farm, both the husband and the wife have to mutually depend upon God. In fact, the whole family is interdependent in its trust toward God. This is natural because farmers understand that the outcome of all their work totally depends on God. It is God who sends the sunshine and the rain. Plowing, planting, weeding, pruning, and fertilizing are futile if God does not send favorable weather.

Farmers know in a very organic way how much of life depends utterly on God. This produces a natural spirituality even in the non-spiritual. Even the nonbeliever has an innate sense of living before the face of either a cruel or benevolent god. In fact, much of our United States history was imbued with a sense that "God was watching" and judging our collective behaviors. This attitude was primary until about 150 years ago, at which time folks started to move from farms to cities.

When that happened, we did not just lose the farms. We lost the sense of dependent spirituality. In the agrarian model of marriage, this sense of loss can be regained. Husband and wives can pray together that God would bless their primary enterprise, which is their marriage and family. They can pray knowing that success or failure is in His hands. Together they can live life as if they are fully dependent on God (which they are in actuality). It allows couples to not be so anxious about every little thing.

So many issues in marriage are beyond the couple's control, from whether they are able to have children or not, to where they live, to whether they each can find optimal employment, to how well their children will grow up. As couples pray about these, and other issues, they can make decisions knowing all actions are performed before the face of God. Decisions are made within a moral framework—always asking, "Does this decision please God?" The shared priority is not primarily financial success, it is the shared priority of glorifying God through their marriage and family.

Teamwork

Marital success requires a certain set of values and those values can be readily discovered by considering what it takes to run a successful farm. Primarily, it requires a team effort. Someone has to milk the cows…early. Someone has to work the fields while someone else needs to cook the food. Someone has to hold the ladder while the other nails the shingles over the door lintel. I mention this because when my wife and I were working on our family's cabin one summer, my wife neglected to have someone hold the ladder for her and she took a dramatic tumble (she was not seriously hurt). That was painful for her, but a source of humor later on. We took that event as a lesson in the need to work as a team.

On the farm, a husband and wife have work together on their own land to reap a harvest. The work is too great for just one person. The teamwork required by farm life naturally produces communication. If we are to successfully work together, we need to talk, plan, and coordinate all that must be done.

In modern non-agrarian model families, very little communication is needed. Everyone lives in his or her own self-propelled orbit and occasionally one member will share some of what is going on in their world. Yet, regular sharing is needed for the sake of relationship. Wives often come to my counseling office complaining of a lack of communication. This may reflect a model that is not built on teamwork.

The most pure expression of Genesis 2 is the image of a man and a woman working blissfully in the garden together before the fall. They work shoulder to shoulder, in a way no farm animal or domestic pet can do. The couple shares an intimacy that is tied to the land as they work together before the face of God. Their futures are tied together in this enterprise, and they need each other.

Glimpses of this kind of teamwork exist in most contemporary marriages when they plan their wedding, their honeymoon, and settle into their first home. Often there is much teamwork around the birth of a first child, but then as newness of these events recedes, the issues of life begin the inevitable pulling apart. Unless the couple adopts a teamwork conceptualization, separateness begins to creep in like weeds in an unattended field.

Occasionally, a couple will create a life that emphasizes teamwork (just like a farm), such as when they own a business or their own ministry; or when they share a common goal, such as caring for a special needs child, or the promotion of an athletic or artistic prodigy. Some fortunate couples may have the means to pursue a mutual dream, such as my close friends who bought a boat and spent a year sailing the Caribbean. When a couple works on their marriage like they would if they lived on a farm, then that marriage is often successful.

The agrarian value of team work is not just for the family alone. The farm life requires interdependence. I need my neighbors' help at times. My wife and I cannot raise the barn with just the two of us. This is where the public square and democracy come into play. I may have my own farm and marriage, but my success depends on the success of those around me. Together we raise barns, lend a hand during harvest, fix tractors, provide emergency services, protect one another and help each other raise our children. The agrarian model is a great example of what a community ought to exemplify. In a contemporary context, it might just involve knowing who my neighbors are. The next step will mean sharing in their needs. The breadwinner-homemaker model and the more independent models are self-sufficient from their neighbors and all families suffer from the loss.

Children Are Valuable

Teamwork often extends beyond just a couple who are trying to run the farm. You need children. Children are valued members of the enterprise. The more children, the better. All children are welcome, and when there is a succession of them—the older ones can help in raising the younger ones—this gives them firsthand experience for when they have their own kids. The point is, children are valued and not seen as a financial burden. This mindset is a key point. In the breadwinner-homemaker model, "too many" children means the husband has to work even more hours. And successive children can be unconsciously devalued by other family members.

The general attitude that children are a burden and not an asset, is completely contrary to the Bible. Those children who were unconsciously devalued are not likely to want to expend a lot of personal capital on their parents when they get to the nursing home. If you are reading this, and are a primary breadwinning husband, you may object to the previous statements. You might say, "I work outside of the home and make plenty of money. My wife stays at home and we can easily afford the four children that we have. We do not devalue them."

That may be true, however my point is that for many in the breadwinner-homemaker camp, children are eventually connected to a price tag. In contemporary American society, two children are always welcomed, but once you pass that society begins to ask, "Can you really afford another child?" Some more progressive minded folk might even reject the idea of an "extra child" or more than two children as simply irresponsible. They might question whether the earth's resources should be drained in terms of environmental impact and overpopulation. In the Agrarian model, every child is a financial asset, never a deficit.

Most of my college students are shocked to realize children were seen as the purpose of marriage until recently. Michael Sandel, the Harvard professor I mentioned previously, talks about the *telios* or purpose of marriage being the raising of children. Think about it, why did most young people get married in the past? To have children. This was especially true for traditional females who dreamed of maternal bliss. When marriage is divorced (pun-intended) from its purpose, there is no readily identifiable replacement. Why even get married? In the past, sexual relations were sanctioned through marriage. Children were born into a presumably stable two-parent home. Women were protected by a covenant agreement that they would not be left alone with the children. Today, none of these rationales hold.

Sex apart from marriage is seen as a cultural norm among single adults. Marriage is unnecessary in their minds. More recently, the trend to cohabitate makes marriage unnecessary even when children are the product of living together. High divorce rates contribute to general acceptance of the idea that children do not require married parents (after all, many are now raised by single moms). When the connection between marriage and procreation is lost, the meaning of marriage is also lost. This has led to the most common contemporary understanding or model of marriage—the self-fulfillment model.

To illustrate to my students how radically the cultural view about marriage has changed in the United States, I often start with the example of marital change in the small country of Scotland. In 1991, the average age for marriage was 27 for males and 25 for females. More recently, the average age of marriage has been delayed to 32 for males and 30 for females[24].

People who wait until later in life to get married believe children can be had after careers are established or not at all. Since having children is not a driving motivation, many couples cohabitate. This results in a birth rate of under two children per couple. Unique to Scotland is that many young people emigrate, or leave their small country to move to England or elsewhere. This leaves Scotland with very few "wee little ones" running around. Culturally, the Scottish are not big on adoption to make up the difference. In 2001, the entire country had only 468 adoptions. The net outcome of this trend over time is that Scotland will no longer be able to sustain itself. Cultures with low birth rates eventually die out.

I used this illustration to point to the problems of decreasing birth rates in Scotland, however data from the last major U.S. Census reveals that we are following Scotland's trend. The median age for a man's first marriage was 28.2 years in 2010, up from 26.1 in 1990. The median age for a woman's first marriage was 26.1 years in 2010, up from 23.9 in 1990. A related trend noted in the U.S Census is that the number of unmarried couples living together has increased in the United States to 12% of all couples, up from 10% in the year 2000. Hence, we have the Scotland phenomenon.

Since childbirth can be delayed or raised outside of marriage, the connection between marriage and having children is cloudy. This leads to confusion about the purpose of marriage.

When the Supreme Court of Hawaii considered the legality of gay marriage quite a few years back (they were the first State to initially allow gay marriage), the judges were most concerned about the impact of gay marriage on children. Psychological testimony seemed to support that idea that there would be no adverse psychological impact, so the judges allowed gay marriages to proceed. My point is not about gay marriage, but that judges knew that any change to marital law would first have to pass a test related to impact on children – at that time, child welfare was tied to the purpose of the marriage. That fact (the connection between the purpose of marriage and children) has been lost in recent years. The people of Hawaii subsequently passed a referendum opposing gay marriage and Hawaii later adopted civil unions for gay couples.

Many states have since passed laws legalizing gay marriage, so the effect is that many children will be raised in nontraditional settings. Also, the majority of gay marriages do not produce children (though some adopt children or obtain children through surrogacy), so the purpose of marriage is further distanced from procreation. High divorce rates, cohabitation, and legalizing of gay marriage serves to redefine marriage. It is no longer about children and children are not valued. The public square no longer works hard to pass legislation to favor traditional families. In fact, it is quite the opposite.

High abortion rates support my contention that contemporary society does not value children. Each year about 20% of all pregnancies end in abortion. Since the ruling of Roe v. Wade in 1973, there have been slightly more than one million abortions each year. There were 1.21 million abortions in 2010. The counter argument is that society does value children in that non-aborted children are more desired and can be reasonably supported by mothers when they choose to give birth. But that logic is far from the agrarian model. Instead children are seen in terms of a cost analysis benefit.

By not valuing and promoting marriage as tied to procreation, less children will be born. The nursing home metaphor will then be lost. Contemporary models of family life do not promote increased childbirth rates. As of this writing, the U.S. Government has debt levels in the trillions of dollars. This debt will be passed on to future generations. If there are significant declines in the population level, then the system will collapse financially. This most likely means that programs like Medicaid and Medicare that make nursing homes possible will also be in trouble. There may be no nursing homes around to complete the narrative we began at the start of this chapter.

Children are essential to our nation's existence.

Democratic Leadership in the Home

Leadership in farming communities has often been associated with "patriarchy" or male rule. Patriarchy is a four letter word in academic communities where it is painted in very harsh and negative terms (the father as tyrant model). However, that particular view of patriarchy is not the biblical understanding of male leadership as discussed earlier in this book, and is it not part of the agrarian model. The agrarian model requires teamwork, real communication, and mutuality. With those elements in place, someone must be in charge, and most farmers are not authoritarians.

Farmers need the support and backup of their wives who seem more like a "right hand man" than in the breadwinner-homemaker model. In fact, a strong woman with a normal woman's body is welcomed. It would be hard to imagine most runway models doing a lot of work on the farm. Because farming is a joint enterprise of the husband and wife, there is much more natural sharing and mutuality than when either goes off to the work force. Roles do tend toward traditional hierarchies with the parents being "in charge" of the children, but even then, children work together with their parents to sustain the family farm.

In modern families, there is plenty of money to go around, but children have no role in the enterprise. Children are simply consumers and never producers. Often the parents spend the majority of their free time feeding the consumer needs of the children and roles easily get reversed. I often see children who demand their parents to buy them things, drive them to friends' houses, and enslave them in their extracurricular activities. Life revolves around the children's needs rather the enterprise of the family in which all are participates.

In the agrarian model, decisions have to be calculated in terms of its overall effect on family priority. The breadwinner-homemaker model is a life without margin. The agrarian model has its own time and seasons and margins built in, however the leader will at times have to call the members to task in those seasons when everything must be put on hold so the crops can be harvested.

The agrarian model supports mutuality, but it is also important that there be a responsible agent for making final decisions. The husband is seen as the head of the home. This is especially true with regard to spiritual leadership where it is commanded in the Bible. This is democratic in the sense that in functional families the husband leads with the consent of governed. When they married, she voted to let him lead her in terms of the final say in most matters. Of course if he is unwise or a sinful leader, the wife has a responsibility to voice her concerns.

The agrarian model is not a top-down authoritarian leadership, but leadership that works together to make sure the boat is on course. The husband provides desired and needful leadership, but not forced and coercive leadership. This type of democratic leadership makes account for those under the executive level. It takes input from the trusted executive officer as well as the governed (the children).

A farm or family enterprise cannot successfully be a one-man operation. I have already noted that Harvard professor Michael Sandel has said this type of government in the family and then in the community led to the very unique concept of American democracy. It is very unlikely that most of the founding fathers of the United States were tyrants at home while sacrificing their lives to rid tyranny from the public square. Strong male leadership creates strong and healthy families, especially when he has a strong wife right by his side.

Much Less Focus on Entertainment

Healthy families, like those on the farm, make deliberate choices in their use of time. They are busy doing things that matter. Whether a sole provider family or a dual income earner family, the children are often left to watch television, play video games, or consume other forms of media. According to video expert Jane McGonigal, by age 21 boys have spent 10,000 hours gaming, most of it in isolation[25]. Data from the Neilson Company indicates that children on average are viewing more than 28 hours of television per week. However, what is even more startling, the Kaiser Family Foundation found that when you add to television viewing all other forms of media such as video games, cell phones, and computers, you end of up with an average of 7 hours and 38 minutes of media usage per day!

The agrarian model encourages children and families to read books and play games together. Rather than being authoritarian micromanagers, agrarian parents allow their daughters and sons to play outside. Even major cities have parks and green space in which children can run, play, and breathe fresh air. In the agrarian model, "safety concerns" which are the forefront of a sensationalistic media, are given a backseat to living naturally. Many of today's young people are so captured by media consumption or by their parent's fear of letting them play outside that they become completely disconnected from nature.

This phenomenon has been described by Richard Louw as Nature Deficit Disorder[26]. By not being outside, children suffer from a lack of imagination development, certain types of cognitive growth, and health benefits that come from just breathing fresh air. And they fail to appreciate the planet God made for us. It is somewhat amusing that kid's television programming is often nature-based and supports causes to help save the environment—an environment in which they have no firsthand knowledge. This was not so in the original agrarian families where there was that intimate connection with the land. Modern agrarian families look for ways to get children away from media consumption and make deliberate choices to go parks or just be outside together.

Non-rigid Gender Roles

When men left the farm to go to work in factories and businesses, wives were obligated to stay home with the kids. This is not an ideal situation—not because the woman is at home, but because the husband is far removed from his family. It is also not a biblical arrangement because fathers have an obligation to be involved in the raising and teaching of their children. Like working the farm, the care and instruction of family needs to be a true team effort. The arrangement where the wife is obligated to be home with the children played a large part in sparking the feminist complaint about traditional family life. Feminists saw the rigid role structure as undesirable when that was the only option available to women.

The Bible is full of the non-rigid gender role models for women. The Proverbs 31 woman is praised because she works in the marketplace to support the family enterprise. She is a woman who is in charge over others. Deborah led Israel, including going into battle. Abigail spoke her mind to David. Ruth and Esther are other examples of strong women who were also willing to be submissive for the sake of others. In the New Testament this does not change. The early church is founded with the help of strong women who play significant leadership and supporting roles.

More than half (56%) of today's college graduates are women[27]. Many of these women grew up with Title IX legislation, which means they were not only good students but they were involved in some type of athletics. Today's young women are bright, educated, and fit. While making progress in a career after college is priority for many young women, family life is also desired even if it seems to be an incompatible goal. They desire to marry and have children (at some point). They just are not attracted to rigid gender roles in which their only option is to stay home with the kids while their husband works.

But if she knew about the agrarian model, she might be attracted to that because she and her husband would work together in the enterprise of marriage and family. She might be the one who works full-time and brings in the most money, while the husband has a less demanding job and can run the kids around or she might choose to stay home to be with her children when they are young and then she and her husband can determine how much time each of them can spend in the workforce.

Ideally, they can have a family enterprise, such as a family business, even home-based, in which both parents have access to the children during the day. The key to this discussion is not about who works full-time and who doesn't, but the biblical concept that woman was originally created to work side-by-side with her husband. She was a helper like none other—the original right hand woman. Her physical strength was not as great as his, but whatever strengths she brought to the table were welcome. If a woman was physically strong that too was an asset, not a deficit as dictated by modern Western ideals about women's bodies. A physically strong woman was not something that society wanted to reduce in Photoshop. Men needed woman to lend them real hands and real bodies. Many Christian models still portray women as weak and needing to be rescued. When the apostle Paul calls women "the weaker vessel," he is simply stating a fact that women in those days needed protection. That was and continues to be a need that church has had to meet in society when women are disadvantaged. In present society, males need the support of strong females. This does not change his role as leader of the home, but women can play a supporting role in the family in many different ways.

My son and I went for a six-mile run one morning around the 40-acre farmland plots that are common to Northern Michigan. The weather was cool even for August. This was in a rural area, so some of the route was paved and some was gravel. We talked about the Canadian Geese, the Seagulls, the loud Sandhill Cranes, and a host of other birds that circled above and swooped down on the newly cleared hayfields. It was a slow run, but we picked up our pace considerably when chased consecutively by a Collie, a large sheepdog Terrier, and an old birddog as we passed various farm houses. For the record, the sheepdog was the most persistent.

The fields reflected beautiful shades of green with prominent brown hay bales that seemed artistically spaced on the farmer's canvas. Red barns and tractors provided visual contrast to the sea of green. As we ran and talked, we noted a large field almost completely covered with a bright yellow wildflower weed. The color comparison was pretty, but this farmer's field only produced four bales of usable hay. Our wise Uncle Virgil explained to us later that those weeds were almost impossible to eliminate once they take hold.

The analogy to family life was instantly two-fold in my mind. Not all families are the same—some are highly fruitful and show the marks of labor and care, and some are neglected. The neglected family can produce something that looks good, but really it is almost useless. Second, similar to what Uncle Virgil had said, once bad habits develop, they are hard to eliminate. As you survey the farm that is your family, how would your family appear if someone were to jog by? What impression would your family give a visitor to your home?

The major source of weeds is that most non-agrarians approach marriage in a manner that is inherently selfish. The question they ask is, "What am I getting out of this relationship?" The agrarian also expects to receive a bountiful return on his labor, however he asks a very different question, "How I can best plow in this relationship to get a return?" The agrarian is concerned about his role in terms of timing, the amount and type of seeds to sow, creating the right conditions in the soil, and the amount of fertilizer to apply. The non-agrarian is passive in the relationship. He does little work, but still expects a big return.

The agrarian knows he has a large role to play in cultivating the relationship. Not just when the couple is courting, but day in and day out over the course of marriage. The agrarian gets his hands dirty, does what needs to be done for his spouse to grow. In real life, the analogy breaks down, because the husband and wife work the soil of their marriage together and then corporately wait for God to produce the fruit. There is no such thing as passive agrarians, except for agrarians with unsuccessful marriages and farms full of weeds.

Real Life Examples

In case you are still thrown by the use of farming terms, you could also think of this model as the "family enterprise" model. The husband or wife has a job with flexible hours that may bring in the largest income or they are able to be home in some type of work-at-home business. Then the other spouse is able to work part-time or be at home supporting the home-based business. The point is that both the husband and wife are committed to being around the home and being around when the children are home. Additionally, the husband and wife purposefully spend more time together.

Here are some examples of the agrarian/family enterprise model, all based on families I personally know with good marriages and who are raising successful families:

- **Scott and Amy.** They own a small farm with crops and horses. They also own a trucking business that they run together off-site and at a home office. They are around the house whenever the kids are home. Their kids go to a rural public school. They are very involved with their kid's lives and those kids have lots of chores on the farm.
- **Roger and Susan.** Susan works as an attorney with flexible hours. Roger has a computer-based business. Roger acts as "soccer mom" and transports the kids to a Christian school. Both are very involved with the kids and are home when the kids are home.
- **Phil and Donna.** Donna teaches classes online and Phil does customer service online from home. They also have several internet-based businesses to bring in extra income. They are both at home and homeschool their kids.
- **Rick and Brenda.** He works as a college professor with a flexible schedule and Brenda works part-time as a nurse. Both Rick and Brenda take on homeschool instruction duties.
- **Henry and Lisa.** He is a successful developer/entrepreneur and is often around the home for homeschool instruction and domestic support. He is also the home athletics director (PE teacher). Lisa works as a homemaker and together they are a raising an excellent crop of 12 children.

Notice how family enterprise is what drives all of these examples. Additionally, when agrarian families are engaged in professions that bring in more income they make deliberate choices not to max out in their careers. Enough is enough. Additionally, they place a high degree of mutuality in both domestic support and instruction of the children (whether they homeschool or not). Finally, because the focus is on life at home, and not just career or financial success, there is a deliberate movement away from materialism.

Four Things a Wife Can Do to Help Her Husband

Being a woman is a terribly difficult task, since it consists principally in dealing with men.
—Joseph Conrad

The other day I saw one of the sexiest things I think I have seen in long time. It was not on cable TV and it did not involve an actress or model. It did involve a couple I know. The couple is an attractive pair in their forties and they have several children. We were out in public and the husband was talking about something rather mundane. His wife was leaning in and staring rapturously at her husband as if hanging on every word he was uttering. She had this look on her face that conveyed her husband must be the most interesting man in the world. That was sexy. Especially since I knew that their 25 years of marriage hasn't always been easy.

The husband had to learn to love his wife as outlined in this book. It did not come automatically to him and the respect the wife now has for her husband was not easily obtained either. It took work for both of them. However, now whenever the husband is talking, his wife responds as if he is someone who deserves respect. The effect is quite astonishing. Showing respect is one thing that truly strikes a deep vein with men. It can help them more than most women can appreciate. I guess that is why the Bible tells husbands to love their wives and for wives to respect their husbands. Love and respect are gender targeted drugs that reach into the deepest parts of our psyches.

This book was written to help husbands. I did not write a book for women and marriage because I believe men and women are different. They are physically wired differently, they handle emotions differently, they respond to things differently, they are attracted to different things, and they think differently. Note that I did not say one is superior to the other. They are just different.

Since I really believe in gender differences, I have no credibility in trying to tell a woman what she should do with her marriage. As a husband, church elder, Christian professor, and psychologist I believe I have the authority to speak to men, but I limit what I can say to wives to the most obvious points. From experience, I would tentatively propose that there are at least four things a wife can do to help her husband. She can show him respect, she can appreciate his physical nature, she can be assertive, and she can pray for him.

Show Respect

We live in uncivilized times. We also live at time in which society demands fairness and equality. I believe the concept of equality has somehow morphed into the notion that is unfashionable to treat certain people with respect. One of your greatest American values is that of "fairness." Everyone should be treated the same, hence showing respect violates the rules of equality, and being respectful makes you strangely un-American. Therefore, only racists, anti-feminists, and those who are stuck in the past are worried about issues of respect. Talking heads shout over one another on TV. People cut in front of each other in stores and on the highway. Authority figures are the most vilified and political differences allow everyone, including Christians, to mock the president of our country. All rude behavior is justified because we tend to only care about our self-interests. And yet, men crave respect. Respect is a good thing and not the enemy of equality. If you meet the president or any person of important stature, you should act respectfully.

Husbands should love and value their wives and this means treating them with respect. Wives should understand that showing respect to her husband does not diminish her value or right to equality—it's just that your spouse should be more valuable to you than other males in your life. God made men to crave respect and it is smart to show respect for your husband. Showing respect for your boss, professor, neighbor, and showing less respect for your husband is the road to marital discord. Secretly, many wives probably believe that by treating their husbands with respect, they are somehow giving up their right to equality. My advice is that it need not be that way.

Growing up, males face constant competition and comparison—so much so that it becomes ingrained into their thinking patterns. Men often evaluate themselves is terms of accomplishments, sports ability, and financial success. On the playground, and in the board room, there are winners and losers. Many men feel like losers because no matter how good they are in sports, or how much money they make, there is always a comparison group that does better. A man who runs long distance races at a six-minute pace can tell you about a bunch of guys who run at a five-minute mile pace. A man who has a few million dollars in the bank can tell you about a bunch of guys with tens of millions of dollars.

Successful men often have great fears and insecurities. Guys who have been in the military have faced a constant barrage of rankings and evaluations, and generally the theme was not about how praiseworthy they have been. So there is deep longing for respect. They are not usually seeking verbal praise—they may have rarely received verbal praise, but that is not what they long for, rather they long for an attitude of respect.

This is where submission comes into play. No one should be a slave to another, however as Christians we voluntarily submit by showing a measure of respect. A wife is not expected to do everything a husband requests, but she can adopt an attitude that this man is the most important human being in her life. She can show respect by listening, agreeing (when possible), and having an attitude that her spouse is of utmost importance in her life. She can put what he says and desires high on her list of priorities. She can ask the Lord to help her obey Ephesians 5:25 which says, "Wives respect your husbands."

Appreciate His Physical Nature

My dentist was a man's man, a real adventurer type. He flew his own plane, surfed and sailed in the ocean, rode a motorcycle, and was incredibly fit. He grew up in Fort Lauderdale, Florida when it was a small beach town, spending his youth outside doing all kinds of physically demanding activities. Later in life, he had three beautiful daughters. He did not allow to them to watch TV, instead he sent them outside to play just like he had done as a boy.

When his daughters got in fights with each other and could not resolve an issue, he moved the furniture in his living room and cleared a space on the floor so they could have wrestling matches to determine the outcome of the conflict. Wrestling as a way to resolve problems is a very male thing. And though it is not a very ladylike way to resolve an issue, you would have to admit that only a guy would even come up such a thing.

A friend of mine worked for a man who owned a large construction company in South Florida during the construction boon days. When this man had financial disagreements with owners and sub-contractors, he would occasionally go out to parking lot and resolve the issue through the use of fisticuffs. Fighting as a way to resolve problems is a very male thing. Men have a physical nature.

A man should never resolve disagreements with his wife through any type of physical display or even threat of physical dominance. Male domination is the opposite of what God wants in a marriage. Having made that clear, there are ways that a wife can help her husband by understanding this deeply ingrained physical nature.

Many men respond better to touch than verbal parlays. In heated exchanges, a husband should learn to just walk away and a wife should learn to not chase after him. In less heated exchanges, women should remember that certain words are "fighting words" so they need to be assertive, but also use common sense with their choice of words. Using certain words that are humiliating to a man when obviously he cannot respond physically creates tremendous frustration.

When things are going well, it is great if a woman can increase opportunity for physical contact. A wife can simply sit close to him on the couch. Just being close to him increases a release of testosterone in his system. So, jump on his lap sometimes when he is in his favorite chair. Make contact and touch him occasionally, especially while talking. This lets him know when something is important. Also, allow him to touch you when you are in the kitchen. Don't get all bent out of shape over physical contact. This sends him the wrong message.

If possible, do outside physical activities with your husband. Walking is great, but so is any sport you can play together. Even working in the garden together can be a way of bonding because it is a physical activity you do together.

Finally, remember that men have a need for sexual release. Women avoid touch because it may be a signal for sexual relations. A good marriage will have lots of physical contact that does not always lead to sex. This works on cycle just like women have monthly cycles. Of course, men's cycles look for sex more than once a month! Every couple just has to work through how often sex will occur, but the aspect of a man's physical nature cannot be ignored. Most husbands are open to increasing physical contact in various ways with an understanding that a wife may be open to contact if she believes such contact will not have to lead to sexual activity. This needs to be addressed directly, because physical contact is simply a good thing in a marriage.

She Can Be Assertive

Men are not mind readers. But we do have short attention spans. We get easily distracted. This means you will have to repeat yourself. While husbands should become leaders, it is helpful if our wives assert themselves. Direct opinions and reminders are good things. What men do not like (nor does any person) is being talked down to or reminded of past failures.

> Bill, how could you forget to pick up the milk?
> Bill, I already told you we were going to the Martin's house tonight.
> I should not have to repeat myself to you.
> I am not going to tell you what I want for my birthday.
> You should know.

When a wife refuses to express her needs and wants because she believes those wants and needs have been communicated already, then her refusal is not assertive, but passive aggressive. It is a way to get back at her husband for not listening. If not listening is the problem, then a wife should let her husband know they need to talk about listening. This should be brought up in a positive way and not a condemning manner.

> Bill can we talk sometime?
> Sure.
> I would like to come up with ways that will help me tell you things so you will listen. Sometimes I feel like you don't hear me and I have to repeat myself. What suggestions do you have?

Much of communication is a matter of good timing. The biggest takeaway from the popular *Men are from Mars and Women are from Venus* books is, "Men need cave time when they get home." Meeting anyone with a crisis as soon as he walks in the door is never good. If you can, be happy to see your husband when he gets home. Give him a hug and kiss. Then find a time free of distraction and communicate. Ask him if he is ready to listen. If he says no, then demonstrate respect and ask him when would be a good time. If he says tomorrow, then wait till tomorrow. Once you have his attention, start by telling him positive news or praise him for something. After that, without criticism or sarcasm, calmly state your wants, your needs, and your honest opinions, and then leave it at that. Be direct and allow him to pick up on your lead. This is how men talk to each other. They don't use a lot of extra verbal output and fluff. To quote a very old detective show, "Just the facts, ma'am."

As a marriage counselor I have seen many women stew over bad feelings for years because their wants and needs were not being addressed. Women have some responsibility in this area to communicate. Hurt feelings are not a reason to quit communicating. If it is really important enough to be upset over, then after some prayer and reflection, it's time to bring up the matter again. At some point it could be mutually agreed upon that you and your husband are not going to sell your home and move by your mother (or whatever the issue) but this needs to be brought up until it is resolved.

An unresolved want or need is an excellent reason for which to seek some professional counseling. This allows the couple to discuss the issue openly in front of a third party. Some of my most successful sessions have been with couples discussing what they should do with family members (a child or older parent) when the wife needed to be heard, but the husband wouldn't listen.

It is important to keep in mind that being assertive as a wife is not counter to male spiritual leadership at home. The Bible commends Abigail, the wife of David in the Old Testament. What did she do? She went around her doltish husband and asserted herself directly before David. This was a special case, because David was God's representative on earth at the time, and we do not have the same authority structure today. Jesus is our representative. If a wife a believes Jesus wants her to obey Him in some manner, then she needs to assert herself. Abigail's assertive manner was never the problem. The woman described in Proverbs 31 is a very assertive and successful woman. The book of Genesis says woman was created to be man's helper. That means that man needs your help, and it requires assertiveness.

She Can Pray for Him

As we've discussed, as prophet, priest, and king of the home, husbands should be praying for their wives, and family, daily. Wives already seem to know they are supposed to do this. When a wife prays specifically for her husband, there is a special kind of synergism or spiritual power that takes place. God is delighted to honor the prayers of a praying wife. A husband is uniquely blessed when he knows he has the prayers of his wife behind them.

When both the husband and the wife pray for each other every day, then there is the potential for a marriage made in heaven. The intimacy that mutual prayer creates is much stronger than the typical worldly ways of creating bonding. If communication is about timing, then prayer is about consistency. A wife will see results in her marriage if she commits to pray for her husband every day. Evidence for that last statement can be seen in the success of the book, *The Power of a Praying Wife*, by Stormie Omartian.

When a wife prays, dynamic things happen. Just read the reviews on Amazon about Omartian's book and you will get the idea. Or order the book for yourself.

There are two great models of women in the Bible who pray and receive miraculous results. In the Old Testament, Hannah prayed fervently for a son, and then she gave birth to Samuel who became the spiritual leader of Israel at the time of Saul and David (1 Samuel 1:1-28). In the New Testament, the childless Elizabeth prayed at an "advanced age" and gave birth to John the Baptist, the cousin of Jesus (Luke 1:13). God pays attention when faithful women pray. He is most happy to answer prayers that are directed at the blessing of a husband or a family. Finally, there is an indication in the New Testament that a wife can "sanctify" her husband and family and possibly even lead a non-believing husband to salvation. A passage to support idea is found in I Corinthians 7:14 which states, "For the unbelieving husband is sanctified by his wife." How does this happen? It happens when she lives respectfully before her husband, which implies that she is praying for him (see also I Peter 3:1).

I said above that a wife needs to assertively help her husband because whether he knows in or not, he needs the help. But he also needs something even more—he needs prayer for protection from temptation. For most men they need protection from sexual temptation, but all of us face temptations of various forms. A wife can help her husband when she understands that others out there are aware of his physical nature and desire for respect and those forces do assert themselves negatively toward every husband. Most importantly, a wife's prayers are one of the best defenses against the power of those temptations.

APPENDIX:
Selected Marital Resources

Recommended Christian Marriage Books

Marc and Grace Driscoll (2012*). Real Marriage: The Truth About Sex, Friendship and Life Together.* Thomas Nelson.

Timothy Keller (2011). *The Meaning of Marriage: Facing the Complexities of Commitment with the Wisdom of God.* Dutton Adult.

R.C. Sproul (2004). *The Intimate Marriage: A Practical Guide to Building a Great Marriage.* P&R Publishing.

Douglas Wilson (1995). *Reforming Marriage.* Canon Press.

Recommended Marriage Books – not explicitly Christian

William F. Harley (2001). *His Needs Her Needs: Building an Affair-Proof Marriage.* Revell Books.

Pat Love and Steven Stosny (2007). *How to improve your marriage without talking about it.* Broadway Books.

Books on Communication

Henry Virkler (2009). Speaking the Truth in Love. Xulon Press.

Resources for Marriages on the Verge of Divorce

Diane Medved (1990). *The case Against Divorce.* Ivy Books. (This book is an oldie but still a good warning against divorce – the material in Barlow is more current).

Brent A. Barlow, Ph.D. *Marriage at the Crossroads: Why Divorce is often not the Best Option (Rationale, Resources, References).* http://ce.byu.edu/cw/fuf/Archives/2002/BrentABarlow.pdf

Resources for Problems with Pornography and Purity Issues

Tim Challies (2012). *Sexual Detox*. Cruciform Press.

Mark Laaser (2004). *Healing the Wounds of Sexual Addiction.* Zondervan Publishing.

Harry Schaumburg (2009). *Undefiled: Recovery from Sexual Sin, Restoration for Relationships.* Moody Press.

William M. Struthers (2009*). Wired for Intimacy: How Pornography Hijacks the Male Brain.* InterVarsity Press.

Douglas Wilson (1999). *Fidelity*. Canon Press.

Recovering from Affairs

Dave Carder (2008). *Torn Asunder: Recovering from an Extramarital Affair.* Moody Publishers.

John Nieder and Thomas Thompson (2010). *Forgive and Love Again: Healing Wounded Relationships.* Harvest House Publishers.

Books for Depression, Anger and Significance

David D. Burns (2000). *The Feeling Good Handbook.* Plume Books. (This is not a Christian book but it has helped many people treat depression and anxiety).

David P. Murray (2010). *Christians get depressed too. Reformation Heritage Publishers.*

Robert D. Jones (2005). *Uprooting Anger: Biblical Answers to a Common Problem.* P & R Publishing.

Robert S. McGee (2003). *The Search for Significance.* W Publishing Group.

Praying for your spouse

Andrew Case (2009). *Prayers of an Excellent Wife: Intercession for Him.* Create Space: Independent Publishing Platform.

Stormie Omartian (2007). *The Power of a Praying Woman.* Harvest House Publishers.

REFERENCES

1. http://pastors.com/cohatitation-no-longer-a-divorce-risk-not-hardly/
2. Andrew J. Cherlin (2006). *Public and Private Families: An Introduction.* McGaw-Hill.
3. Brent A. Barlow, Ph.D. *Marriage at the Crossroads: Why Divorce is often not the Best Option (Rationale, Resources, References).* http://ce.byu.edu/cw/fuf/Archives/2002/BrentABarlow.pdf.
4. "All Scripture references are from the New King James Version unless otherwise noted." The Holy Bible, New King James Version copyright © 1982 by Thomas Nelson, Inc.
5. Les and Leslie Parrot (*2006*). *Saving Your Marriage before it Starts: Seven Questions to Ask before and after You Marry.* Zondervan Publishing.
6. Leo Bascaglia. http://www.goodreads.com/author/quotes/27573.Leo_Buscaglia
7. Armand Nicholi (2003). *The Question of God.* Free Press.
8. Walter Trobisch (1971). *I Married You.* Quiet Waters Publications.
9. Leo Bascaglia. http://www.goodreads.com/author/quotes/27573.Leo_Buscaglia
10. "This general idea comes from Douglas Wilson". Douglas Wilson (1995). *Reforming Marriage.* Canon Press.
11. Palm Beach Post, "Redbook cover is a leap of Faith" (July 24, 2007)
12. Dabbs, J.M., Jr., Ruback, R. B., & Besch, N. F. (1987). *Male saliva testosterone following conversations with male and female partners.* Paper presented at the American Psychological Association Convention.
13. U. S. Senate Hearing on Science, Technology and Space: The Science Behind Pornography Addiction, November 18, 2004.
14. Mattox, W.R., "Aha! Call it the revenge of the church ladies," *USA Today,* February 11, 1999
15. Robert H. Schuller (2006). *Believe in the God who Believes in You.* Orient Paperbacks.
16. Robert S. McGee (2003). *The Search for Significance.* W Publishing Group.
17. Douglas Wilson (1995). *Reforming Marriage.* Canon Press.
18. CDC data from 2011. *http://www.cdc.gov/nchs/data/databriefs/db76.pdf*

19. Antidepressant use:
    http://meps.ahrq.gov/mepsweb/data_files/publications/st206/stat206.shtml
20. *Paul Biegler (2011). The ethical treatment of depression: Autonomy through psychotherapy. Cambridge MA: MIT press.*
21. Hymnal.net (2013).
22. Many of my ideas for this chapter come from Michael Sandel. See Michael J. Sandel (1998). *Democracy's Discontent: American in Search of Public Policy*. Harvard University Press. And many of his more current publications.
23. http://thepioneerwoman.com
24. *Age at first marriage Scotland: http://www.gro-scotland.gov.uk/press/news2011/rg-on-population-changes.html*
25. Jane McGonigal: Gaming can make a better world. Video on TED.com
26. *Reference: Kay Hymowitz(2011). Manning Up: How the Rise of Women has Turned Men into Boys. Basic Books.*
27. Richard Louv (2008). *Last Child in the Woods: Saving our Children from Nature Deficit Disorder*. Algonquin Press.

ACKNOWLEDGEMENTS

It takes a community to raise a barn and a lot of encouragement to write a book about marriage. If I have forgotten to mention anyone I am truly sorry and I remain grateful for anyone who has taken even a small interest this project. The following folks were special encouragers and resources:

Two individuals who asked often over many years - Greg Kelchner and Damon Palmer.

Two great men who got the ball rolling – Robert G. Barnes and James M. Vigorito.

One couple who finally helped me get published - Brent and Katrina Gray.

Two couples who encouraged – Pat and Cherie Fitzgibbon and Andrew and Shelly Pond.

Two guys who are very book smart – Ron Benson (pastor/writer) and Lee Warren (editor).

Two real friends – Don Marks and Tim Ladd, each one helped tremendously in their own way.

Two spiritual leaders – Dave Dorst and Tom Hendrikse (my pastors).

And one couple who actually thought the book was good - Joe and Gail Michelini.

CPSIA information can be obtained at www.ICGtesting.com
Printed in the USA
LVOW12s2057200813

348670LV00002B/9/P